Application Coordination in Pervasive Systems

INFORMATIONSTECHNOLOGIE UND ÖKONOMIE
Herausgegeben von Christian Becker, Wolfgang Gaul,
Armin Heinzl, Alexander Mädche und Martin Schader

Band 50

Verena Elisabeth Majuntke

Application Coordination in Pervasive Systems

Bibliographic Information published by the Deutsche Nationalbibliothek
The Deutsche Nationalbibliothek lists this publication in the Deutsche Nationalbibliografie; detailed bibliographic data is available in the internet at http://dnb.d-nb.de.

Zugl.: Mannheim, Univ., Diss., 2012

Library of Congress Cataloging-in-Publication Data

Majuntke, Verena Elisabeth, 1980-
  Application coordination in pervasive systems / Verena Elisabeth Majuntke.
    pages cm — (Informationstechnologie und Ökonomie, ISSN 1616-086X ; Band 50)
  "Zugl.: Mannheim, Univ., Diss., 2012"—Title page verso.
  Includes bibliographical references.
  ISBN 978-3-631-64304-4
  1. Application software. 2. Ubiquitous computing. I. Title.
  QA76.76.A65M325 2013
  004—dc23
                                                        2013020992

D 180
ISSN 1616-086X
ISBN 978-3-631-64304-4
© Peter Lang GmbH
Internationaler Verlag der Wissenschaften
Frankfurt am Main 2013
All rights reserved.
PL Academic Research is an Imprint of Peter Lang GmbH.

Peter Lang – Frankfurt am Main · Bern · Bruxelles · New York · Oxford · Warszawa · Wien

All parts of this publication are protected by copyright. Any utilisation outside the strict limits of the copyright law, without the permission of the publisher, is forbidden and liable to prosecution. This applies in particular to reproductions, translations, microfilming, and storage and processing in electronic retrieval systems.

www.peterlang.de

Abstract

Our future environment will be managed by a multitude of different pervasive systems. A pervasive system consists of users and devices which cooperate to provide functionality to the users. The provision of functionality is realized by pervasive applications. A major characteristic of pervasive applications is their context-interactivity. On one hand, pervasive applications are context-aware and can adapt themselves to changing context. This ability enables them to provide their functionality in different configurations. On the other hand, pervasive applications have the ability to influence and change the context themselves. A context change can be caused implicitly as a side effect of employed resources or explicitly through the use of actuators. Due to the context-interactivity, problems are likely to occur when two or more applications are executed in the same physical space. Since applications share a common context and interact with it, they can have a direct impact on each other.

The described problem is defined as an interference in this thesis. An interference is an application-produced context that impairs the functionality provision of another application. To manage interferences in pervasive systems, a coordination framework is presented. The framework detects interferences using a context model and information about how applications interact with the shared context. The resolution of an interference is achieved through a coordinated application adaptation. The idea is based on the assumption that an alternative application configuration may yield a different context interaction. Thus, the framework determines a configuration for each application such that the context interactions do not interfere. Once a configuration is found for each application, the framework instructs applications to instantiate the selected configuration, resolving the interference.

The framework is unique due to three design decisions. At first, the framework is realized as a cross-system coordination layer in order to allow an integration of arbitrary systems. Secondly, the integration of applications can be achieved through the extension of existing systems while preserving their system characteristics. Thirdly, the framework supports a generic interface to integrate arbitrary resolution strategies in order to allow the customization of the framework to the needs of different pervasive systems. The thesis introduces the theoretical concepts of the framework, presents a prototypical implementation and evaluates the prototype and its implemented concepts through extensive measurements.

Acknowledgements

First of all, I would like to thank my supervisor „Chef" Prof. Dr. Christian Becker. Throughout all the years, Christian gave me the freedom to develop and follow my own research interests. He always knew how to keep the motivation up even in cases of setbacks. Thanks to Christian the years of my PhD studies were an exceptionally positive experience. I thank my second supervisor Prof. Dr. Martin Schader for his time and the effort he put in to enable my graduation in 2012. In a casual conversation in October 2012 he decided to give me the chance to receive my PhD degree before the end of the year 2012. This did not only mean a lot of work for me but also a time commitment from his side. I also would like to thank Prof. Dr. Armin Heinzl who filled in on my Rigorosum on very short notice. I am very grateful to my postdoc Dr. Gregor Schiele who always had an open ear and a lot of time to profoundly discuss my research and various aspects of life. I already miss our coffee breaks. Fortunately, Gregor has become a good friend and the conversation times are not restricted to the office. Furthermore, I thank my colleague Richard Süselbeck. Richard was one of the first PhD students at Christian's chair just like me and we shared an office. The English theater will always remain a legend. I also thank Laura Itzel (now Krammer). We worked together for a little while and I am glad we became friends and not only colleagues. A big "Thank You" also goes to all Wifo II members for making everyday-work in the group such a great time, to Kerstin for taking care of us and for being the good soul of the chair and to Markus, the ruler of the IT landscape. I thank Andrew Lefoley for proof-reading my thesis and for supporting me whenever needed. Finally, I thank my husband Matthias who fortunately knows the challenges of writing a thesis and who had to endure my ups and downs and my sister Dinah who has always known how to turn my bad days into good ones.

Contents

1 Introduction   1
    1.1 Pervasive Computing 1
    1.2 Business Applications 2
    1.3 Motivation 3
    1.4 Research Aim 5
    1.5 Contribution 6
    1.6 Structure 8

2 Background   11
    2.1 Pervasive Systems 11
    2.2 Applications in Pervasive Systems 14
       2.2.1 Classification Criteria 15
            2.2.1.1 Context Type 16
            2.2.1.2 Adaptation Level 17
            2.2.1.3 Adaptation Control 18
            2.2.1.4 Architectural Approach 19
       2.2.2 Classification of Existing Approaches 19
       2.2.3 Pervasive Applications 24
    2.3 Interference in Pervasive Systems 26

3 Coordination: System Model and Requirements   31
    3.1 System Model 31
    3.2 Application Coordination 33

ix

3.3	Requirements		36
	I	System Integration	36
	II	System Autonomy	36
	III	Runtime Coordination	37
	IV	Application-Specific Interferences	37
	V	Minimal User Distraction	38
	VI	Strategy-Based Coordination	38
	VII	Correctness of Interference Detection	39
	VIII	Completeness of Interference Resolution	39

4 Related Work   41

4.1	Interference	41
4.2	Application Coordination	44
	4.2.1 Interference Detection	45
	4.2.2 Interference Resolution	48

5 Framework for Application Coordination   53

5.1	Design Rationale	53
	5.1.1 Cross-System Coordination Layer	54
	5.1.2 Extension of Existing Application Systems	55
	5.1.3 Strategy-Based Application Coordination	57
5.2	Framework Overview	59
5.3	System Extensions	64
	5.3.1 Context Configuration	65
	5.3.1.1 Context Ontology and Context	66
	5.3.1.2 Interference Specifications	68
	5.3.1.3 Context Influences	76
5.4	Application Coordination Framework	78
	5.4.1 Interference Detection	78
	5.4.2 Interference Resolution	81

5.4.2.1	Interference Resolution Plan Computation	82
5.4.2.2	Interference Resolution Plan Problem as CSP	85
5.4.2.3	Algorithms for Constraint Satisfaction Problems	86
5.4.2.4	Discussion	89
5.4.2.5	Coordination Strategy Realization	91

6 Application Coordination in Pervasive Systems   97

- 6.1 System Characteristics ... 97
- 6.2 Smart Environments and Smart Peer Groups ... 99
- 6.3 Requirements ... 101
  - IX Coordination Efficiency ... 101
  - X Best-Effort Application Coordination ... 101
  - XI Minimal Additional Load for Resource-Poor Devices ... 102
  - XII Availability of Application Coordination Functionality ... 102
- 6.4 Component Placement ... 102
  - 6.4.1 Interference Detection ... 104
  - 6.4.2 Interference Resolution ... 108
- 6.5 Dynamic Application Coordination ... 111

7 Protoype   115

- 7.1 Coordinator Overview ... 115
- 7.2 Context Configuration ... 118
- 7.3 Configuration and Application Management ... 120
- 7.4 Context Management ... 121
  - 7.4.1 Context Ontology ... 121
  - 7.4.2 Context Model ... 123
- 7.5 Interference Detection ... 125
- 7.6 Interference Resolution ... 128
- 7.7 Coordinator as a Service ... 130

8 Evaluation   133

8.1	Memory Requirements and Overhead	133
8.2	Performance Measurements	137
8.2.1	Critical Path	137
8.2.2	Interference Detection	140
8.2.3	Interference Resolution Plan Computation	143

9 Conclusion and Outlook   153

9.1	Conclusion	153
9.2	Outlook	155

Bibliography   157

List of Figures

2.1	Smart Environment (SE) [Sch07]	12
2.2	Smart Peer Groups (SPG) [Sch07]	13
2.3	Interferences	27
3.1	Multi-Platform Pervasive System	33
5.1	Cross-System Coordination Layer	54
5.2	Overview: Application Coordination Framework	60
5.3	Interface: Instructable	64
5.4	Input Matrix of Applications and Context Configurations	92
5.5	Pruning Process	96
6.1	Overview: Data Access	103
6.2	Interference Detection: Component Placement	105
6.3	Interference Resolution: Component Placement	109
6.4	Application Coordination: Component Placement	112
6.5	Coordinator Setup Process	113
7.1	UML: Coordinator Overview	116
7.2	UML: Context Configuration	118
7.3	UML: Coordinator Management Tables	119
7.4	Context Ontology Extract	122
7.5	UML: Context Model	123
7.6	UML: Interference Detection	126
7.7	UML: Interference Resolution	128

7.8	Coordinator as BASE Service	131
8.1	Overview: Application Coordination Process	138
8.2	Measurement Results for *BasicInterferenceDetection*	141
8.3	Interference Resolution: $r = 1$, $i = 2$	145
8.4	Interference Resolution:: $r = m/2$, $i = 2$	146
8.5	Ordering vs. Non-Ordering	150

List of Tables

2.1	Classification Criteria for Pervasive Applications	15
2.2	Overview and Classification: Pervasive Applications	21
5.1	Overview: Logic Expressiveness	71
5.2	Overview: Logic Complexity	72
5.3	Example: Interference Resolution Problem	83
7.1	Internal Structure of the Context Model	125
8.1	Memory Requirements: Coordinator Classes	134
8.2	Memory Requirements: ContextConfiguration and ContextList	135
8.3	Memory Requirements and Overhead	135
8.4	Performance Results for the Critical Path	139
8.5	Basic vs. Optimized Interference Detection, $|CI/IS| = 9$	143
8.6	Test Case 1: Required Steps and Time, $m = 4$	147
8.7	Test Case 1: Required Steps and Time, $m = 8$	147
8.8	Test Case 2: Required Steps and Time, $m = 4$	148
8.9	Test Case 2: Required Steps and Time, $m = 8$	149

List of Tables

1. Introduction

This chapter serves the purpose to give an overview of the thesis at hand and the addressed problem statements. At first, it describes the vision of pervasive computing and discusses the trends towards pervasive computing and its importance in the industrial sector. Subsequently, the problem of interferences in pervasive systems is identified and the need for their management is motivated. The motivation is followed by the definition of a research aim and a summary of the contributions of this thesis. The introduction of the research aim closes with an overview of the thesis structure.

1.1. Pervasive Computing

The notion of *Ubiquitous Computing*, or *Pervasive Computing*, was first introduced by Mark Weiser in 1991. In his essay *The Computer for the 21st Century* [Wei91], Weiser described his vision of the human-computer interaction. He predicted that the future human environment would be pervaded by a multitude of information processing devices. Being equipped with respective hard- and software, these devices will be able to form networks and to cooperate in the interest of their users. Through their cooperation they would provide functionality to users assisting them seamlessly in their everyday tasks. The explicit human-computer interaction would transform into an implicit use of the functionality the networks provide. As a result, the user's environment would become intelligent, sensing the user's need and aiming at an optimal user support at any time and anywhere.

    The vision of Mark Weiser has brought forth a multitude of approaches that contribute to the realization of pervasive computing. Early approaches in this area were projects such as Aura [GSSS02] or Gaia [RHC+02] which addressed a variety of aspects in pervasive computing and yielded system software for their realization. More than twenty years later, a truly pervasive system as described in Weiser's vision is yet to be realized. However, the trend towards pervasive computing has become visible in different areas. One of the areas which is discussed in the following is the business sector.

1.2. Business Applications

In 2006, a study entitled "Pervasive Computing: Trends and Impacts" [BSI06] was developed by order of the German Federal Office for Information Security (BSI). The study was conducted in cooperation with VDI/VDE Innovation und Technik GmbH, Fraunhofer Institute for Secure Information Technology and Sun Microsystems GmbH. One goal of the study was to identify trends in pervasive computing and to analyze impacts on the industrial sector. The results of the study reflect the knowledge of international experts that was gathered through a comprehensive online survey and a variety of interviews. The following discussion on pervasive computing in the industrial sector and the observations are extracted from the study.

The study revealed that a variety of areas exist in which "pervasive computing is already recognisable and is very likely to play a decisive role in the future" [BSI06, p. 22]. An area in which the trend towards pervasive computing is evident is the sector of production and logistics [BSI06, Section 4.1, pp. 23-25]. Nowadays, IT-based controlling and monitoring systems are an integral part of production-specific and logistical systems. The aim of such systems is the optimization and automation of production, transport and supply along the entire supply chain. The integration of physical objects is realized by attaching artifacts to the objects providing them with digitally ascertainable data. In earlier systems, the use of bar code was the prevailing standard. However, a disadvantage of bar code was its requirement to physically access the artifact to retrieve the stored data. The use of RFID, in contrast, enables a remote access to the artifacts and thus the data. Thus, the tracking and tracing of objects without the need of additional physical actions has become viable. While a complete automation and optimization has yet to be achieved, a trend towards intelligent and autonomous systems is obvious.

1.3. Motivation

E-commerce has been identified as another area in which pervasive computing has become recognizable [BSI06, Section 4.6, pp. 30-31]. An enabler for e-commerce has been the fact that today's users can typically be identified through pervasive computing objects such as their smart phones. The exploitation of user profiles and preferences provides a large potential for user-tailored marketing and location-based services [VMG+01]. The use of location-based services has contributed to the sharing of costly products such as bicycles and cars. Depending on the user's location, the availability of such objects can be determined and their use can be precisely recorded and billed. As a result, such systems enable the shared utilization of capital-intensive objects and can provide an attractive business model to users.

Another example is the area of medical care [BSI06, Section 4.7, pp. 31-33]. Medical and health-related systems have been identified as a large application area for pervasive computing. The optimization and automation of core processes in this area promise a large potential for cost reductions. As an example, pervasive systems could be employed to monitor patients at home to avoid long-term stays in hospitals for observation reasons. Likewise, the state of patients with chronic illnesses could continuously be monitored in order to develop an optimal treatment plan and to adapt it if necessary. Besides the cost factor, this also has the potential to improve the patient's quality of life. Instead of being bound to the hospital bed, the treatment could be realized in an environment familiar to the patient.

1.3. Motivation

The results of the BSI study reveal that pervasive computing is increasingly present in the human's daily life. The promise of pervasive computing is the optimization and automation of processes core to the respective area. In the area of logistics, core processes can be all processes involved in the management of stock such as tracking of pallets and ordering on demand. In the context of smart homes this could be the realization of any tasks to ease its user life. Conceivable examples are the adjustment of the temperature to its user's needs or the redirection of a phone call to the room the user is currently in.

The vision of Mark Weiser has brought forth a variety of research work that aims at the realization of pervasive computing. Technically, pervasive computing is realized by a *pervasive system*. A pervasive system consists of users, devices, and the physical space they reside in. In order to provide functionality to users, *pervasive applications* are executed. A pervasive application is a distributed application which makes use of resources and capabilities currently available in the pervasive system. To provide their functionality anytime and anywhere, pervasive applications are *context-aware* and *adaptive*. According to Dey [Dey01], "context is any information that can be used to characterize the situation of an entity". The entity may be a user, a specific location, or any kind of object that may have an impact on the application's behavior. This context-awareness allows the application to incorporate the context information into configuration decisions. The adaptivity enables the application to adjust to changing contexts, pursuing an optimal configuration at all times. As a result, a pervasive application is able to continuously provide functionality in different functional configurations.

While pervasive applications have been specifically designed to adapt themselves to changing environments, the application's ability to *influence* the environment and thus to change the context itself is often neglected. Such a context influence can either be produced implicitly as a side effect of employed resources or explicitly through the use of available actuators. As a consequence, the relationship between an application and the context is bidirectional. The context influences a pervasive application and vice versa. The fact that applications interact with the context and not only react to context changes makes them *context interactive*.

When an application is run in isolation, its ability to influence the context can be neglected. The execution of multiple applications, however, leads to new challenges if the applications are executed in the same physical space. The challenges arise from the fact that applications *share* the physical environment as common context and *interact* with it. One one hand, they react to changes in the context by adapting themselves. On the other hand, they change the context according to their needs. As a consequence, pervasive applications are directly related with each other via the context they share.

Consider the following example: User Anne is in the living room reading on her e-book reader. In order to provide a good contrast, her application has turned on the lights. After a while Bob enters the living room. His intention is to watch a movie on the projector installed in the environment. To do so, his application closes the blinds and turns off the light to provide the optimal atmosphere for a movie. Bob's application clearly has an impact on Anne's application. The changing of the light level impairs the functionality provision of Anne's application. In this scenario, the e-book application has two options to deal with the context change. It can 1) adapt the context according to its need again, i.e. turn on the light and open the blinds or 2) adapt itself, i.e. by redirecting its output to another device for example. The first option may result in both applications taking turns adapting the context. The second option may lead to a situation where the e-book application cannot provide its functionality anymore.

The described problem is referred to as an *interference* throughout this thesis. An interference is an application-produced context that impairs the functionality provision of another application. The problem can be reduced to the fact that applications which are executed in the same physical space *share* and *interact* with a common context. As a consequence, they can have a direct impact on each other through the commonly shared context.

1.4. Research Aim

The fact that interferences can occur becomes more problematic given that future user environments are likely to comprise not only multiple applications within a single system, but also multiple pervasive systems. With the continuous development of pervasive computing, it is very unlikely that the world will be managed by only a single system. Instead, a variety of different pervasive systems will exist in parallel. As a consequence, pervasive applications which are executed in the same physical space are likely to interfere with each other even if they are executed in different pervasive systems. Ideally, the occurrence of interferences should be avoided to enable the unobstructed provision of functionality by multiple applications in the same physical space. In practice, however, the context-interactivity is one of the major characteristics of pervasive applications. As a consequence, interferences cannot be avoided and thus must be detected and resolved at runtime to allow an undisturbed pervasive system experience. The goal of the thesis at hand is to develop an approach to manage interferences in terms of their detection and resolution. The proposed solution must be able to manage interferences across multiple systems. It should consider the needs of its users and handle interferences in their interest.

Up to the present, the management of interferences as defined in this thesis has not been addressed in its entirety. Some research work exists which addresses the management of subsets of the interference problem , e.g. [KMW03], [MD06], [SHW05], or [RC03]. Other work focuses on the realization of frameworks to detect and resolve problems between multiple applications such as [MD06] and [BRK06]. However, their work remains on a theoretical level and has not been developed to handle the addressed problems at runtime. Further approaches exclusively focus on the task of interference detection, e.g. [PLH05], [SW09], and [AKM06], or specific interference resolution strategies, e.g. [JCL11], [HME+06], and [SW05]. In summary, none of the existing approaches is able to handle the problem of interferences as addressed in this thesis.

1.5. Contribution

The contribution of this thesis is a coordination framework that manages interferences between applications in pervasive systems. The management is split into two tasks, interference detection and interference resolution. For interference detection, applications are required to provide information to the framework about their context interaction in their current functional configuration. Based on this knowledge and a context model, interferences can be detected. For interference resolution, applications are required to specify and provide interactions for alternative functional configurations. If the framework detects an interference, it determines interference-free context interactions for each application to resolve the interference. The applications are then requested to instantiate the respective functional configuration that complies with the context interaction. Thus, a coordinated application adaptation is performed. Specifically, the contributions of this thesis are:

1.5. Contribution

(I) Interference Model and Detection: The thesis analyzes the problem of interferences in detail and introduces a formal model for interferences based on monadic predicate logic [Löw31]. Based on the interference model, the problem of interference detection is discussed and two algorithms, a basic statement evaluation and an optimized version, are presented.

(II) Interference Resolution Plan Computation: The first step of interference resolution is the computation of a respective plan. Based on the model of interferences, the problem of interference resolution plan computation is modeled as a constraint satisfaction problem (CSP) and the suitability of algorithm classes for CSPs is discussed for pervasive systems. Furthermore, a heuristic that uses information about an application's involvement in an interference is introduced realizing an informed backtracking algorithm to compute an interference resolution plan.

(III) Design: The framework is designed to be tailored to pervasive systems which can be heterogeneous, dynamic and open with respect to devices, users and pervasive applications. For this purpose, the framework design is subject to three decisions:

  (a) Cross-System Coordination Layer: The framework is designed as a cross-system coordination layer. It coordinates the interaction of pervasive applications with the shared context across different system software. For the realization, the requirements towards application systems are kept at a minimum and abstract from details specific to a particular pervasive system. Besides these requirements, integrated application systems are treated as black boxes.

  (b) Extension of Existing Systems: The minimal requirements described in the previous design decision are realized through extensions of existing application systems. For this purpose, the concept of a context configuration is introduced. The context configuration extends a functional configuration with the specification of its context interaction. Furthermore, an adaptation interface is introduced that allows the framework to request the instantiation of a configuration computed by the application itself.

(c) Strategy-based Application Coordination: A variety of aspects can be considered when applications are coordinated in order to maintain an interference-free system state. For this purpose, the framework realizes a generic interface for the use of arbitrary resolution strategies. This allows to customize the framework for the needs of different pervasive systems.

(IV) Development and Evaluation: A prototypical realization is developed that implements the theoretical concepts of the framework. Furthermore, extensive evaluations are conducted in order to show the utilizability of the coordination framework in practical pervasive systems.

(a) Component Placement and Communication Sequences: System characteristics that have an impact on the practical realization are identified and discussed for general pervasive systems. Based on the findings, recommendations for the placement of components that compose the framework and the points in time when data should be exchanged are given.

(b) Prototype and Measurements: The prototype COMITY is developed that implements the concepts of the application coordination framework. Furthermore, measurements are conducted to assess the quality of the prototype and the concepts it implements. For this purpose, the memory requirement and the overhead it causes are analyzed. Furthermore, the algorithms for interference detection and resolution are evaluated.

1.6. Structure

The remainder of the thesis is structured as follows: Chapter 2 provides the preliminaries for the contributions of this thesis. It introduces the concept of pervasive systems and discusses the notion of pervasive applications to realize functionality in such systems. Furthermore, it identifies major characteristics of pervasive applications and classifies existing approaches along these criteria. The result is an overview of existing approaches and their commonalities yielding a definition for pervasive applications used in this thesis.

1.6. Structure

Finally, the problem of interferences is discussed as situations which are likely to occur when multiple applications are executed in the same physical space.

Chapter 3 defines the research question of this thesis. For this purpose, the chapter first introduces a system model describing the target system for which a solution is to be developed. Subsequently, it presents the concept of application coordination as the idea to manage interferences in the target systems and defines the goals of this thesis. The chapter closes with the identification and analysis of requirements towards the approach to be taken. The requirements tailor the approach to the pervasive systems and thus refine the research goal.

Chapter 4 discusses related work. At first, related problems and definitions similar to the notion of interferences are analyzed. Then, related work with respect to application coordination is addressed. The chapter introduces comprehensive approaches which address the entire process of application coordination. Finally, existing work with respect to the isolated tasks of interference detection and interference resolution is evaluated.

Chapter 5 presents the framework for application coordination as the approach to handle interferences in the targeted pervasive systems. To start with, the chapter discusses the major design decisions for the framework. Subsequently, it gives an overview of the framework, its compositional parts and describes the mode of operation. The overview is followed by an elaboration on how existing systems need to be extended in order to allow their coordination through the framework. Finally, the tasks of interference detection and interference resolution are addressed. After a thorough analysis of the underlying theory, respective solutions are discussed and developed.

Chapter 6 analyzes the realization of the theoretical application coordination framework for practical pervasive systems. The practical realization covers the component deployment and the points in time when communication is performed. To develop a viable approach, the chapter first identifies system characteristics which have an impact on realization decisions. It then analyzes general pervasive systems with respect to these characteristics. Based on the findings, decisions on component placement and their interaction to realize application coordination are presented. Finally, the dynamism of pervasive systems is addressed and an approach for its handling is discussed.

Chapter 7 presents the prototype COMITY. The prototype implements the concepts described in Chapter 5 and 6. It gives an overview of the classes and discusses the details of the implementation. Finally, the realization of the coordinator for an existing system – the middleware BASE – is presented.

Chapter 8 evaluates the prototype presented in Chapter 7. The chapter analyzes the memory requirements of the coordinator and discusses its overhead in relation to BASE. Furthermore, the chapter conducts performance measurements with respect to the critical path of application coordination and the algorithms implemented for interference detection and resolution.

Chapter 9 closes the thesis with a summary of the results and an outlook on future work.

2. Background

This chapter provides the conceptual preliminaries of the thesis at hand. Section 2.1 presents a general introduction to the notion of pervasive computing and its realization through pervasive systems. Section 2.2 discusses the concept of pervasive applications to provide functionality in such systems. At first, classification criteria for pervasive applications are identified and described in detail. Subsequently, existing approaches are classified along the criteria and characteristics of general pervasive applications are summarized. Finally, Section 2.3 analyzes the problem of interferences in pervasive systems and gives the definition of interferences in the context of this thesis.

2.1. Pervasive Systems

Mark Weiser's vision of *Pervasive Computing* describes the existence of an omnipresent network of information processing devices assisting humans in their everyday tasks. However, the pure existence of information processing devices in a person's daily environments does not suffice. In order to be a truly pervasive, helpful system, these devices need to be able to form networks, communicate, and cooperate with each other. It is in this cooperation that users can be best supported in their daily life. The environment needs to become smart, assisting the user in her tasks anytime and anywhere.

The technical realization of pervasive computing is achieved by a *pervasive system*. A pervasive system consists of a set of devices connected in a network infrastructure, users to whom functionality is provided, and the physical space the devices and users reside in. An example for a pervasive system is an intelligent home that provides assisted living for elderly people. In this example the user is a person with special – and potentially changing – physical needs, the physical space is the living environment of that person, and the set of devices comprises the networked devices designed to assist the user with her needs. Examples of potential functionalities provided include an automated heating and ventilation system, automated visual and/or auditory reminders to take prescribed medicine, an alarm system the inhabitant can access in multiple ways, or even motion-detection devices which can automatically call for help if the inhabitant has had a fall. Further examples of pervasive systems include smart office environments that support employees with their daily working tasks or a smart factory in which workers are aided throughout the entire production cycle.

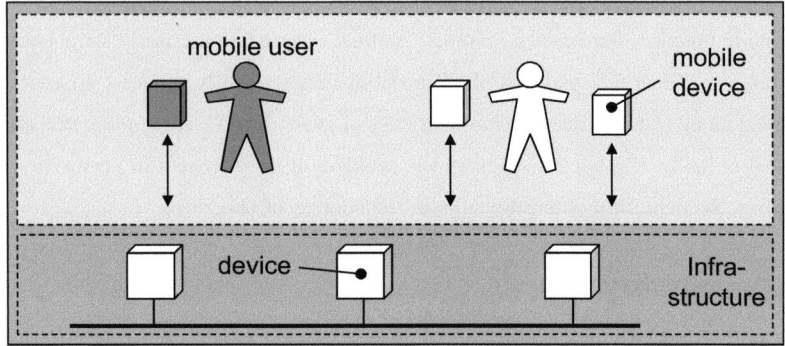

Figure 2.1.: Smart Environment (SE) [Sch07]

Pervasive systems can be realized based on two concepts, a *smart environment* or a *smart peer group*. Figure 2.1 illustrates the concept of a smart environment. The approach is characterized through the existence of a predefined infrastructure of devices. These devices may be stationary such as a desktop computer or may be mobile devices being carried by a user such as a PDA. The resourcefulness of the single devices may range from powerful processing devices such as a server down to resource-poor devices such as sensors. Due to the existence of stationary devices, the physical space of the pervasive system is determined through the location of the infrastructure. The devices in a smart environment and the functionalities they offer are typically managed in a centralized manner. The infrastructure usually contains at least one powerful device which provides

2.1. Pervasive Systems

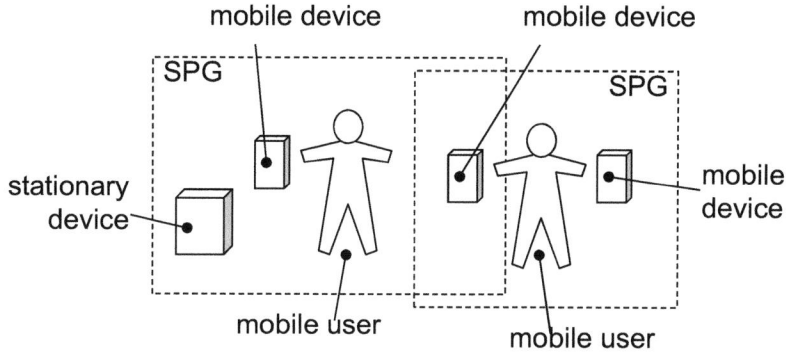

Figure 2.2.: Smart Peer Groups (SPG) [Sch07]

enough capacity to manage resources in the system and to realize functionalities. In order to cooperate, devices in the smart environment are equipped with adequate system software. This also allows for a dynamic integration of mobile devices if the respective system software is present. Smart environments are also often referred to as active spaces [RHC[+]02], smart spaces [Sat01], or intelligent spaces [CFJ03]. Examples in the literature for smart environment based approaches are Aura [GSSS02], one.world [GDH[+]01], Gaia [RHC[+]02], or iRos [PJKF03].

The second concept for the realization of a pervasive system is a smart peer group. The concept of a smart peer group is illustrated in Figure 2.2. A smart peer group is a spontaneously formed network of devices which are in communication range of each other. Devices are able to detect each other and to form an ad-hoc network without the need of user interaction. As soon as a group has been formed, devices can directly interact with each other on a peer-to-peer basis. Thus, in contrast to smart environments, smart peer groups do not rely on a predefined infrastructure. The resources and the functionalities provided by a smart peer group are managed in a decentralized way.

Devices are selected for cooperation based on the assumption that a user prefers to make use of nearby devices [Sch07]. To support this as well as user mobility, devices in a smart peer group are likely to use wireless communication technology such as Bluetooth [Blu] or Wi-fi [Wf] to detect and interact with each other. The use of wired communication technology however is not excluded. The goal to support user mobility also has an impact on the physical space of the pervasive system. The physical space depends on the location of the users and their devices and thus may change over time. As a consequence, smart peer groups are typically user-centric. They form around a user device and move with the user respectively. Similarly to smart environments, devices in the smart peer group need to be equipped with appropriate system software to form ad-hoc networks and to provide functionalities in such networks. Examples in the literature of smart peer group based approaches are BASE/PCOM [BSGR03] [BHSR04] or P2PComp [FHMO04].

2.2. Applications in Pervasive Systems

The provision of functionality in pervasive systems is realized through the execution of applications. Pervasive applications are typically distributed making use of the resources provided by the devices which are present in the pervasive system. In order to determine which functionality needs to be provided to a user in any given situation, applications are *context-aware* [SAW94]. They are able to obtain information about the user and the environment and to incorporate this information into configuration decisions. This information is typically referred to as the *context*. According to the definition of Dey [Dey01] "context is any information that can be used to characterize the situation of an entity". The entity may be a person, a certain location, or any kind of object that may have an influence on the application specifics in a certain situation. As the environment of a user may change over time, applications are *adaptive*. They are able to perceive changes in their execution environment and to adapt accordingly.

A variety of approaches exists which aim at the realization of applications for pervasive computing. Representative and comprehensive classes with respect to the number of approaches are *location-based services* [VMG+01], *context-aware systems* [SAW94] and *pervasive computing applications* [BBG+00]. The majority of approaches which address applications for pervasive computing can be assigned to one of the three classes. While every approach contributes to the realization of pervasive computing applications, the

2.2. Applications in Pervasive Systems

focus of the classes differs. For this purpose, an overview of existing approaches and their characteristics is given in the following. Furthermore, the criteria which have been inferred from a thorough analysis of existing approaches are presented and discussed. Subsequently, the existing approaches are classified along these criteria. Finally, a definition of *pervasive applications* as it will be used throughout this thesis is given. The term pervasive application subsumes the three major classes, location-based services, context-aware systems, and pervasive computing applications into a more general definition.

2.2.1. Classification Criteria

The classification of existing approaches requires a selection of respective criteria along which the approaches can be characterized. An analysis of existing approaches and related literature has led to the selection of different categories as shown in Table 2.1. The criteria can be divided into four broad categories, *context type*, *adaptation level*, *adaptation control*, and *system architecture*. Each category comprises two or more subcategories. *Context type* has three subcategories: *location context*, *technical context*, and *user context*. The adaptation level comprises two subcategories, *system* and *application*, where application itself possesses four subcategories, namely *composition*, *behavior*, *explicit context*, and *implicit context*. *Adaptation control* has two subcategories: *manual* and *automatic* adaptation. The last category, *system architecture*, has three subcategories: *centralized*, *peer-to-peer*, and *hybrid*. The context types and their subcategories are described in detail in the following.

Context Categories	Context Type			Adaptation Level					Adaptation Control		System Architecture		
Subcategories	Location	Technical	User	System	Application				Manual	Automatic	Centralized	P2P	Hybrid
Subsubcategories					Composition	Behavior	Context (exp)	Context (imp)					

Table 2.1.: Classification Criteria for Pervasive Applications

2.2.1.1. Context Type

The provision of functionality to a user in any given situation requires applications to be able to incorporate context information into configuration decisions. The criterion *context type* refers to the kind of context an application is able to retrieve and to process. The retrieval of context can be achieved through a direct access of sensors via a mechanism that may be provided by the system software or through a context server which is available in the pervasive system [BDR07]. The types of context an application makes use of can be split into three classes, namely *location, technical context*, and *user context*.

Location: Location information is any kind of information that is used to identify and define the position of a user in a physical space. A typical example for location information are coordinates in the Global Positioning System (GPS) [GPS]. The use of location models such as [Sat05], [BBR02], and [BZD02] which subdivide buildings into floors and rooms which provide a symbolic reference for locations are also part of this category. Within an indoor space additional techniques, such as infrared, may also be used, to compute the approximate position of a user in a room.

Technical Context: The technical context of an application provides information about nearby and available devices and resources [SAW94]. As a pervasive system is expected to be dynamic the technical context is used by applications to select the devices which are physically close to a user. A reasonable example is that information should be displayed in a user's physical range. A possibility to identify nearby users is the computation of physical proximity based on location information. On the other hand, nearby devices can also be identified searching for devices in wireless communication range.

User context: The last subcategory of the context type is information about the user and her environment. This context type covers information which is not addressed by the former two categories. It may, for example, comprise the activity a user is involved in or the relationships it has with other users in the environment. Furthermore, environmental information may involve information about the physical surrounding of a user such as the noise or the light level of the room the user is present in.

2.2.1.2. Adaptation Level

Applications which realize pervasive computing are adaptive in order to cope with changes in their execution environment and to be able to continuously provide functionality. Thus, the second criterion along which approaches are classified is the kind of adaptation they realize. The analysis of the literature has shown that adaptation can be split into two kinds, adaptation on the *system* level and adaptation on the *application* level.

System: Adaptation on the system level denotes an adaptation of parts of the system software based on which applications are realized. A service that is part of a system software and searches for configurations of an application may for example change the configuration algorithm at runtime depending on available memory and memory requirements. Similarly, a discovery service may employ a power-saving service lookup if the battery of the device the service runs on is low.

Application: The adaptation on the application level can be subdivided into four different subcategories, *composition, behavior, context (explicit)*, and *context (implicit)*. The compositional adaptation refers to the ability of an application to adapt the current set of parts the application is built of. This may for example be necessary if a device which is hosting an active application part becomes unavailable due to user movement. Consequently, the application must find a respective atomic or complex substitute which may be located on one or more other devices in the environment to continue a functionality provision. Behavioral adaptation does not adapt the composition of an application but the way it provides functionality. Behavioral adaptation is usually applied to parts which are in general parameterizable such as the output quality of media. The third adaptation type in this category is explicit context adaptation. Explicit context adaptation refers to the ability of applications to not only sense the context and adapt themselves accordingly, but to actively modify the context according to their needs. This can be achieved through the use of available actuators such as a light switch to adjust the lightning level in a specific room. The last adaptation type is the implicit context adaptation. Implicit Context adaptation takes place if the application modifies the context but does so as a side-effect of its execution. As an example, an application could use speakers in order to provide information via speech instead of choosing a textual output on a display. The output of speech via speakers obviously has an impact on the noise level on the environment. The current noise level however may be information that is considered as context as well. Consequently, an implicit context adaptation occurs.

2.2.1.3. Adaptation Control

Pervasive computing aims at the provision of functionality to users in order to support them in their everyday tasks. A major criterion for the provision is a seamless user assistance allowing the user to focus on her primary task without distraction. Consequently, approaches aim at the automation of context-awareness and adaptation. However, the ability of an application to autonomously make decisions at runtime also requires respective capabilities and a certain amount on information based on which the application can make decisions. In general, the adaptation control can be subdivided into *automatic* and *manual* adaptation control.

Manual: Manual adaptation is realized by a user in the pervasive system. Manual adaptation may be required if the application is not provided with the ability to make decisions autonomously. The success of a manual adaptation however depends on several factors. Obviously, the user performing the adaptation must have a general idea of the application model and which implications an action has on the application. Furthermore, she needs to be able to capture information of the execution environment which is essential for the application and to determine the best possible adaptation. Supporting the user in decision making using an interface such as *iCompose* [DGM+11] can ease those tasks.

2.2. Applications in Pervasive Systems

Automatic: In contrast to manual adaptation, automatic adaptation is performed by the application without required interaction of the user. To realize this task, applications must have access to essential information and to reason and decide on adaptation at runtime. Moreover, the application requires the ability to actually perform an adaptation after a decision has been made.

2.2.1.4. Architectural Approach

The last category in this overview is the system architecture of existing approaches. The system architecture can be split into three classes, *centralized*, *peer-to-peer*, and *hybrid*.

Centralized: A centralized approach follows a client-server model. All services which are required to realize the provision of functionality such as a device discovery, resource manager, or device communication in a pervasive system are provided by a centralized server or infrastructure. In order to realize the task of functionality provision, clients (devices) access and make use of the provided services.

Peer-to-Peer: In contrast to a centralized approach, peer-to-peer based approaches do not rely on a centralized device. System services are realized on a peer-to-peer basis. For example, device discovery is realized by every device in the system. Communication between devices is realized on a peer-to-peer basis and does not require a coordinating centralized communication service.

Hybrid: Approaches which fall into this category are neither purely centralized nor do they follow a pure peer-to-peer based approach but a combination of both. An example of a hybrid approach could provide a centralized device discovery which devices access in order to retrieve devices in the network with whom they interact on a peer-to-peer basis afterwards.

2.2.2. Classification of Existing Approaches

Having defined the classification criteria, Table 2.2 gives an overview of selected approaches and their evaluation with respect to the criteria. The approaches in the table are sorted according to the three previously mentioned classes of approaches, location-based services, context-aware systems, and pervasive computing applications. All of these classes aim at realizing pervasive computing. The table shows a selection of approaches which are representatives for each application class. The listing is not exhaustive. However, the focus lies on the characterization of general classes and not on particular approaches. Thus, the classification of further approaches along the criteria is feasible.

The first row in the column states the criteria based on which existing approaches are analyzed. The first column presents the list of analyzed approaches. A mark in the table indicates that the approach has the respective characteristic. A mark in brackets states that the approach does not explicitly describe this characteristic but is conceivable in general.

Location-Based Services (LBS) comprise the first class of approaches aiming at the realization of pervasive computing. Examples of this class are Cyberguide [AAH+97], GeoNotes [EPS+01], and further approaches ([CDM+00], [BG02], [Pas97]). A location-based service is a functionality which uses information about its user's location as primary context information. Typical applications in this class are those that present location-dependent information to users such as the tourist guides Cyberguide [AAH+97] and GUIDE [CDM+00] or which support the interactive sharing of location-dependent information such as GeoNotes [EPS+01] and e-graffiti [BG02]. If the context, i.e. the location, of a user changes, applications adapt on the behavioral level. For example, they choose the information for the new location and present it to the user. One approach that stands out in the table is the stick-e-notes [Pas97] approach. Stick-e-notes are able to incorporate arbitrary context information in addition to location information to make adaptation choices. With respect to adaptation control, the majority of the approaches offer an automatic adaptation to the extent that a preselection of location-dependent information is made and presented to the user. The final selection, however, needs to be made manually choosing an option from the set of presented possibilities.

2.2. Applications in Pervasive Systems

Approaches	Context Type				Adaptation Level					Adaptation Control		System Architecture		
	Location	Technical	User	System	Composition	Behavior	Context (exp)	Context (imp)	Application	Manual	Automatic	Centralized	P2P	Hybrid
Location-Based Services														
Cyberguide [AAH+97]	X								X	X	X	X		
GUIDE [CDM+00]	X								X	X	X	X		
GeoNotes [EPS+01]	X								X	X	X	X		
E-graffitti [BG02]	X								X	X	X	X		
Stick-e-notes [Pas97]	X	X	X						X	X	X	X		
Context-Aware Systems														
CMF [KMK+03]	X	X	X	(X)	(X)	(X)	(X)	(X)	(X)	(X)	(X)	X		(X)
SOCAM [GPZW04]	X	X	X	(X)	(X)	(X)	(X)	(X)	(X)	(X)	(X)	X		(X)
CASS [DHH07]	X	X	X	(X)	(X)	(X)	(X)	(X)	(X)	(X)	(X)	X		(X)
Context Toolkit [SDA99]	X	X	X	(X)	(X)	(X)	(X)	(X)	(X)	(X)	(X)	X		(X)
Hydrogen [HPL+03]	X	X	X	(X)	(X)	(X)	(X)	(X)	(X)	(X)	(X)	X		(X)
CORTEX [BC04]	X	X	X	(X)	(X)	(X)	(X)	(X)	(X)	(X)	(X)	X		(X)
JCAF [Bar05]	X	X	X	(X)	(X)	(X)	(X)	(X)	(X)	(X)	(X)	X		(X)
Cooltown [BK01] [DGV03]	X	X	X	(X)	(X)	(X)	(X)	(X)	(X)	(X)	(X)	X		(X)
Solar [CLK04]	X	X	X	(X)	(X)	(X)	(X)	(X)	(X)	(X)	(X)	X		(X)
PACE [HIMB05]	X	X	X	(X)	(X)	(X)	(X)	(X)	(X)	(X)	(X)	X		(X)
Active Badge [HHS+02]	X	X							X	X	X	X		
CARISMA [CEM03]	X	X	X	X	X	X				X		X		X
ParcTab [SAW94]	X	X	X	X	X	X	X		X	X	X	X		
Perv. Com. Applications														
Aura [GSSS02] [SG02]	X	X	X		X			(X)		X	X	X		
Gaia [RHC+02] [RC03]	X	X	X		X			X		X	X	X		X
ALLOW [HRKD08]	X	X	X		X					X	X	-	-	-
P2PComp [FHMO04]	X	X	X		X					X		X		X
IRos [PJKF03]	X	X	X		X			X		X	X	X		
REFLECT [SvdZH08]	X	X	X		X	X	X	X		X	X			
Vainino et. al [VVV08]	X		X					X	X		X	X		
OS2 [PPS+08]		X			X				X	(X)	X	-	-	-
One.World [GDH+01]		X			X	X			X	X	X	X		
RUNES [CCM+05]	X	X		X	X		(X)	(X)		X	X			X
3PC [BSGR03] [BHSR04]	(X)	X	(X)	X	X	X	X	(X)	X	X		X		
PECES [HHM09]		X	(X)	X						X		-	-	-
PARM [MV03]		X		X	(X)	X				X	X			

Table 2.2.: Overview and Classification: Pervasive Applications

An interesting observation for this class is the fact that all discussed approaches have the ability to influence context. Even though explicit context adaptation is not realized, the context is implicitly adapted as a side-effect of applications. The presentation of information via speakers that are installed on a user's device, for example, has an impact on the noise level of the environment. In interactive applications, the provision of additional information for a specific location also influences the context for the next user. Lastly, the overview shows that all of the discussed approaches are realized in a centralized architecture. The architecture typically consists of a centralized infrastructure serving a number of client devices. While the infrastructure may provide usable services and information used by these services, the client device retrieves information from the infrastructure based on the location information it communicates.

Context-Aware Systems (CAS) are the second class of applications which realize the provision of functionality in pervasive systems. This class comprises a variety of approaches such as the Context Management Framework [KMK+03], SOCAM [GPZW04], and further approaches ([DHH07], [SDA99], [HPL+03], [BC04], [SAW94], [WSA+95], [Bar05], [CEM03], [BK01], [DGV03], [CLK04], [HIMB05], [HHS+02]). While a lot of a approaches in the class of location-based services aim at the realization of specific applications, a large group focuses on the provision of general frameworks and middleware to support the development and deployment of applications. Using the framework or middleware, arbitrary context-aware applications can be realized. As the approaches do not focus on the application systems but on their support, applications are not restricted with respect to their characteristics. The realization of an application adaptation on all possible levels is conceivable as well as a manual and automatic adaptation support. Furthermore, a hybrid approach can be pursued such that the application may be composed and realized on a peer-to-peer basis, combined with a centralized context retrieval and management. Since the approaches do not explicitly focus on specific applications, arbitrary characteristics are conceivable and thus are stated in brackets.

Approaches in this class which do not focus on the development of an infrastructure but provide systems to actually realize applications are Active Badge [HHS+02], CARISMA [CEM03], and ParcTab [SAW94], [WSA+95]. All of those approaches explicitly support a compositional adaptation on the application level. Furthermore, ParcTab explicitly

2.2. Applications in Pervasive Systems

supports the adaptation of user context. In addition to the adaptation on the application level, CARISMA and ParcTab realize an adaptation on the system level.

Pervasive Computing Applications are the third class represented in the overview. In contrast to the previously discussed classes, approaches in this class focus on the development of system software to build and execute applications in pervasive systems including their support at runtime. Representative approaches in this class are [SvdZH08] and ALLOW [HRKD08] among others ([PJKF03], [PLF+01], [JF02], [VVV08], [GDH+01], [HHM09], [MV03]). Some approaches focus on the development of middleware to realize functionality and to support context-awareness and adaptivity at runtime such as RUNES [CCM+05] or P2PComp [FHMO04]. Others address for example how user goals towards the provision of functionality can be modeled and translated into an executable context-aware and adaptive application at runtime such as ALLOW [HRKD08] or OS2 [PPS+08]. Other comprehensive projects have addressed a variety of different challenges such as the Aura project [GSSS02], [SG02], [JS03], the Gaia project [RHC+02], [CAMCM05], [RCAM+05], [RC01], or the 3PC project [BSGR03], [BHSR04].

The overview table shows that a lot of approaches are able to make use of different kinds of context information. The adaptation focus lies on a compositional adaptation of applications. A lot of approaches also support the adaptation of an application's context. This adaptation is often achieved through the use of actuators which are available given that the approach supports their access. Furthermore, it becomes obvious that the majority of the discussed approaches adapt context implicitly, for example, through the integration and use of respective resources by an active application.

Other approaches in this group realize compositional and behavioral adaptation on the application level while using information about nearby devices as the major context information. RUNES and the 3PC project even provide adaptation on the system level in addition to the application level. Two approaches which stick out in the overview are PECES [HHM09] and PARM [MV03]. Both approaches focus on the adaptation of middleware at runtime and do not address application adaptation. However, both approaches do not adapt their context, neither explicitly nor implicitly.

2.2.3. Pervasive Applications

The preceding overview of existing approaches for pervasive applications has shown that a variety of different systems exist. All of these approaches are context-aware but differ in the kind of context information they are able to incorporate into configuration decisions. Moreover, each approach realizes adaptivity on possibly different levels. One observation that can be made is the fact that a large majority of the discussed approaches are either able to adapt the context explicitly or have the capability to adapt the context implicitly.

In order to provide a common understanding and a basis for discussion, applications which aim at the provision of functionality in pervasive systems are referred to as *pervasive applications* in the following. The concept of a pervasive application subsumes the previously discussed approaches into a more general definition. In the context of this thesis, a pervasive application is defined by three characteristics:

Distribution A pervasive application is typically *distributed*. It makes use of resources and functionalities provided by multiple devices. However, the execution of the application and the retrieval and management of context information on a single device is also conceivable. The set of constituent parts in terms of resources and functionalities that form an application is referred to as the *functional configuration* of the application.

To realize distributed applications, arbitrary application models may be employed. An application model may for example be component-based, task-based, or service-oriented. Its communication may be message based or may be realized via a distributed shared memory. Moreover, the distribution may use a centralized, a peer-to-peer based, or a hybrid approach. In summary, distribution may be realized in a variety of ways.

Context-interactivity A pervasive application is *context-interactive*. The characteristic of being context-interactive consist of two parts, being context-aware and context-influencing. Context-awareness refers to the ability of an application to retrieve context information and to incorporate this information into configuration decisions.

2.2. Applications in Pervasive Systems

The choice on which specific information is considered to be context information depends on the respective approach and application itself. However, for the problem addressed in this thesis, a pervasive application is assumed to at least incorporate location and user context – as discussed in the previous section – in its configuration decisions. The use of technical context is possible but not required. The retrieval of context by an application is not restricted to a certain method. Context information may be provided and accessed via an available context model or through the direct use of sensors in the environment.

As a counterpart of being context-aware, pervasive applications are context-influencing. The characteristic of being context-influencing refers to the ability of a pervasive application to influence and change the context itself. One way to achieve the adaptation of the context is the use of actuators in the environment such as a light switch or a temperature control. This kind of adaption is referred to as explicit context adaptation. Another way to influence the context is an implicit context adaptation. An implicit context adaptation happens when an application uses respective resources which have an impact on the physical environment as a side-effect of their use, e.g. loudspeakers or lamps.

Adaptivity As a last characteristic pervasive applications are *adaptive*. Adaptivity refers to the ability of an application to adapt itself to changing environments. The basis for the adaptivity is the context-awareness. Based on context information, the application can decide how to react to context changes. The self-adaptation can either be a behavioral or a compositional adaptation. In the following, both types of adaptation are referred to as re-configuration of the application. With respect to adaptation control, an automatic approach is assumed. A pervasive application has the ability to make decisions based on the context and to autonomously realize adaptations.

2.3. Interference in Pervasive Systems

The overview of approaches in the last section has shown that research in pervasive computing has yielded a multitude of approaches. The variety in this approaches suggests that pervasive computing is unlikely to be realized by one single and exclusive world-wide system. In contrast, pervasive computing will be realized by a conglomeration of different systems. These systems will coexist and provide functionality to a multitude of users in parallel.

A major challenge that needs to be addressed in the systems that result from the coexistence of multiple pervasive systems is the satisfaction of all users at the same time. Without the provision of additional means, such systems are unlikely to succeed in achieving this goal. The reasons for this and the problems which are likely to occur are analyzed in the following.

Pervasive systems are often designed without considering the existence of multiple users. From the perspective of a single pervasive application, its objective is the provision of functionality to its current user in the best possible way. Based on a variety of information such as user goals, user preferences, context etc. each application aims at an optimal application configuration and context interaction satisfying its user's needs. In single-user environments in which a single application is executed, the adaptation of the application as well as of the context does not pose any challenges. Based on the assumption that an application aims at the satisfaction of the user's goals, the user expects context adaptations to happen explicitly or implicitly.

Consider the example of a smart meeting room in an office environment in which user Anne wants to work on a advertisement video for the company. The video file is located on the notebook she has brought. In order to simulate the official presentation, her pervasive application chooses the projector which is provided by the pre-installed infrastructure as video output device. In order to make the video visible and to provide a high-contrast picture, the application makes use of available actuators in order to set the light level. It closes the blinds and turns off the light. Furthermore, the activity of the room is set to individual work. The application obviously adapts its context according to its needs.

2.3. Interference in Pervasive Systems

The use of the actuators to close the blinds and to turn off the light are explicit context adaptations as well as the activity statement. An implicit context adaptation takes place through the use of the installed speakers to output the audio track influencing the noise level in the environment.

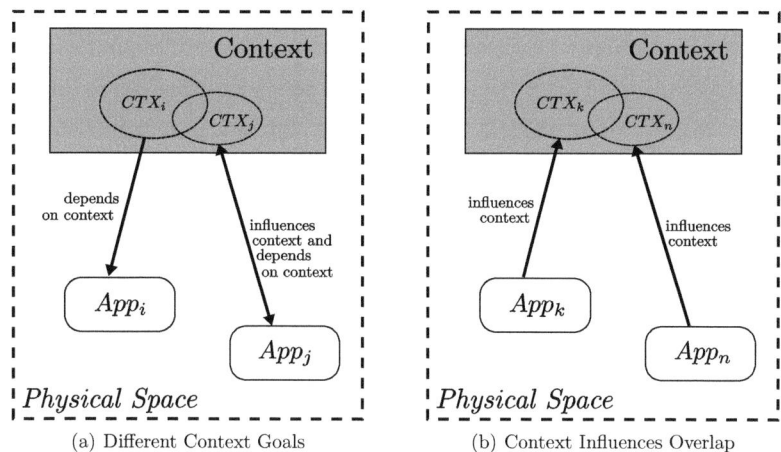

(a) Different Context Goals   (b) Context Influences Overlap

Figure 2.3.: Interferences in Pervasive Systems

While the interaction with the context does not pose any challenges in single-user-single-application environments, challenges arise in multi-user-multi-application environments. The challenges stem from the fact that applications interact with a shared context when they are executed in the same physical space. Figure 2.3 illustrates two possible situations.

Figure 2.3(a) shows two applications – App_i and App_j – which are executed in the same physical space and thus interact with a shared context. Consider the situation in which application App_i has retrieved context information and has based its configuration decision on the current context state. Right after App_i has configured itself App_j is started. App_j discovers that the context does not represent its user's goals in the best possible way. Consequently, it adapts the context according to its needs.

The context which has been adapted by App_j overlaps with the context App_i depends on. Since the context has changed for App_i it is now forced to react. In general, a pervasive application can cope with such a situation in two different ways. First, it can adapt the context again according to its needs by using respective actuators. Especially, as App_i has no means to detect that the context was changed actively by another application, up to the present, it might consider the context adaptation to be a good option. This however may result in a cycle of context adaptations. The re-adaptation of the context will force App_j to react which likewise can choose one of two general options to handle this situation. The problem can be reduced to the fact that both applications have contradicting goals towards the shared context. As a second option, the application can try to adapt to the changed execution environment by adapting itself, e.g. by choosing a configuration based on the new context state. Depending on the resources which are available in the physical space, this process may result in a configuration that is suboptimal for its user. Moreover, no configuration may be found preventing the provision of the functionality.

To exemplify this situation consider the extension of the previously discussed example by another activity Anne wants to pursue. While watching the video Anne decides to take notes on her interactive notepad while studying the advertisement video. In order to provide an optimal context for working with the notepad, the notepad application decides to open the blinds and to turn on the light. The execution of the notebook application clearly has an impact on the video application as it changes the context the video application depends on. The light level in the environment compromises the quality with which the functionality is provided as the video is hardly visible anymore. Since the context has changed the video presentation application is now forced to react. It may either choose to adapt the context again according to its needs or may decide to adapt itself. The adaptation of the context however may yield a context adaptation cycle as both applications obviously have contradicting goals towards the environment. The adaptation of the application itself is likely to not fulfill Anne's goals. The video application could decide to redirect the output to the display of Anne's notebook or to another output device available in the room. However, since Anne wants to simulate the presentation appointment, the reconfigured application is not usable anymore. Moreover,

2.3. Interference in Pervasive Systems

if the physical space does not provide any further output devices, no configuration may be found at all and the functionality cannot be provided.

Another problematic situation that results from interactivity of applications is shown in Figure 2.3(b). As applications have an influence on their physical environment they are likely to interference with each other in the physical space they share. This may lead to a compromise of the quality with which the functionality is provided. This situation is illustrated by applications App_k and App_n who both adapt the context in their execution.

As an example, consider the situation of Anne which was described above. While Anne is watching the video presentation a phone call arrives at her office. Since phone calls are handled by a pervasive application, it retrieves Anne's current location, searches for devices in the location that allow speech input and output and starts the phone call. If both – the video application as well as the phone call application – are executed in parallel without any additional measures, the audio output of both applications interfere with each other. This compromises the quality of both application functionalities. Anne will neither be able to follow the video presentation nor to process the phone call properly.

The situations described above represent examples of a more general problem in pervasive systems. Applications interact with the shared context in terms of making configuration decisions based on context states and adapting the context according to their needs without considering that other applications may be executed in parallel. They are likely to be designed to run in isolation, not taking into account the dependencies other applications have on the shared context. The problem becomes even more general if the pervasive system is assumed to be a multi-user system in which multiple users are served in parallel. While being provided with a certain functionality a user may have requirements towards its physical surrounding. A user that processes a phone call for example may feel disturbed by any other application which has an impact on the noise level such as a music application. The described situations are examples of a general problem which is referred to as *context interference (interference)* as follows:

Definition 1 (Context Interference (Interference))
A context interference (interference) is an application-produced context state which impairs the functionality provision of a pervasive application to a user.

The crucial factor for an interference is the fact that the context is produced by another application in the pervasive system. A pervasive application is designed to be able to cope with context changes and take respective measures. However, in multi-user environments an application-induced context change represents the goals of another user towards the context. If an application's functionality provision is compromised by the created context, a goal conflict between the application evolves. As a result, if the impaired application reacts to the context change, it submits itself to the interests of another user. Since each application represents its own user's needs, this dependence is not tolerable in multi-user environments and needs to be addressed.

To summarize this chapter, a general introduction to pervasive systems and an overview and classification of existing approaches to realize functionality in pervasive systems was given. The classification determined commonalities of pervasive applications and summarized them into a definition of pervasive applications which is used in the context of this thesis. The analysis of existing approaches showed that the majority of pervasive applications are context-interactive. They interact with the context, adapting themselves or the context according to their needs. If two or more applications share a common context, interferences are likely to occur.

3. Coordination: System Model and Requirements

This chapter identifies the research goal of this thesis. At first, Section 3.1 presents the system model which provides a concise definition of the targeted pervasive systems. Subsequently, Section 3.2 discusses coordination as the approach to handle interferences in multi-user pervasive systems. Finally, Section 3.3 infers and analyzes requirements towards a coordination approach from the characteristics described in the system model.

3.1. System Model

The targeted systems are *multi-user* pervasive systems in which a multitude of applications are executed in parallel. A *pervasive system* consists of a set of entities – users, devices which are connected via a network and pervasive applications – and the physical space in which the entities reside. A user in a pervasive system is a human who makes use of the functionality provided by the pervasive system. To provide functionality, the pervasive system comprises a set of heterogeneous devices which are able to form networks. This set may consist of stationary as well as mobile devices which are carried by users. Furthermore, the existence of sensors which are able to capture the state of the physical space as well as the existence of actuators which allow control of objects in the environment is assumed. The resourcefulness of devices may range from powerful devices like a server down to resource-poor devices like a temperature sensor. Functionalities are realized through the execution of pervasive applications. While a user may execute several applications in parallel it is assumed that each application is executed by a single user, the *application owner*. In case a pervasive application is part of an automated system like a building control the owner is said to be the system administrator.

A *pervasive application* is defined by three characteristics as described in Section 2.2.3. Firstly, it is *distributed*, making use of resources and functionalities provided in the pervasive system. Secondly, a pervasive application is *context-interactive*. It uses context information for configuration decisions on one hand while it is also able to change the context itself, e.g. through the use of respective actuators. Thirdly, a pervasive application is *adaptive*. It has the ability to adapt to changing environments by adapting its behavior or its composition resulting in a functional reconfiguration. In addition to the three characteristics, pervasive applications are assumed to be *cooperative* with respect to the management of interferences. The specifics of the willingness to cooperate are discussed in Section 5.3. Furthermore, it is assumed that besides an active functional configuration, each application is able to compute possible alternative configurations as discussed by [GRWK09].

In order to realize pervasive applications, devices are assumed to be equipped with respective system software as discussed in Section 2.2. The concept based on which the respective system software is realized can be a smart environment as well as a smart peer group. The system software provides the basic functionalities in order to manage the pervasive system and to realize pervasive applications. Typical system functionalities are device discovery, resource managers, application configuration, context management, and communication services.

A group of devices which is equipped with the same system software and executes pervasive applications for one or more users is said to be a *uni-platform pervasive system*. The group of devices and users of a uni-platform pervasive system is not fixed and may change over time. Each uni-platform pervasive system independently manages the devices and pervasive applications within the system, involving all tasks which are essential to realize pervasive computing.

An illustration of the targeted pervasive systems – *multi-platform pervasive systems* – is shown in Figure 3.1. A multi-platform pervasive system emerges if two ore more

3.2. Application Coordination

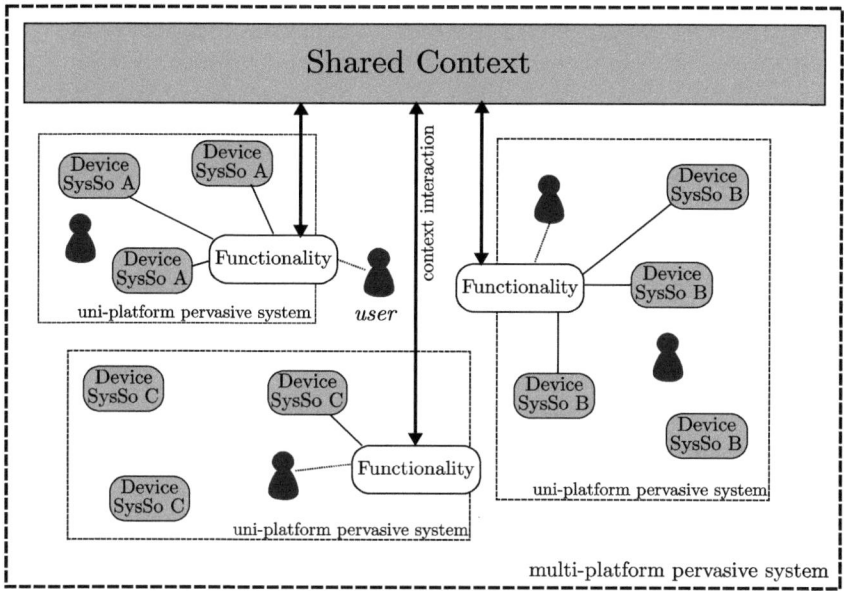

Figure 3.1.: Multi-Platform Pervasive System

uni-platform pervasive systems share a physical space. To determine the physical space of a pervasive system, the existence of a location model like [Sat05], [BBR02], or [BZD02] is assumed. The location model provides a symbolic reference for physical spaces like buildings, floors, and rooms. To ease the discussion in the following, a set of uni-platform pervasive systems is assumed to form a multi-platform pervasive system if their location refers to the same physical space. In the following, the term *pervasive system* always refers to a multi-platform pervasive system as described in this section.

3.2. Application Coordination

In Section 2.3, interferences were identified as a problem that is likely to occur in the targeted pervasive systems. The occurrence of interferences can be ascribed to the fact that applications in a pervasive system *share* and *interact* with a common context. In addition, they lack the awareness that other applications may be executed in parallel.

Moreover, up to the present, the interactions a pervasive application has with the shared context are only known by the application itself. Even if an application was aware of other applications in the environment, it could not exactly determine how these applications depend on and influence the context.

The context-interactivity, however, is a major characteristic of a pervasive application. In order to provide functionality to its user in the best possible way, the application needs to interact with its environment. As a consequence, interferences can hardly be avoided even though this would be the optimal solution. In order to enable the unobstructed provision of functionality to multiple users in pervasive systems, the interaction of pervasive applications with the shared context needs to be coordinated. Coordination in this context means that interferences need to be detected and resolved to maintain an interference-free system state. The existence of an interference indicates the need for coordination. The resolution of an interference realizes the coordination of context interactions. To detect the need for coordination, i.e. an interference, applications need to explicitly define their interaction with the common context. This interaction consists of how an application depends on the current context state and how the application changes the context in its execution. Based on the specification of context interactions, interferences between applications can be detected.

The basic idea to resolve an interference is the coordinated adaptation of applications in the system. According to the system model, pervasive applications are able to provide the same functionality in different functional configurations. The functional configuration determines the interaction of an application with the shared context. Thus, an adaptation of the application may also change the interaction of the application with the context. However, the application will be able to continue the provision of its functionality. As an example, consider a music application which runs on a smart phone and uses speakers which are installed in the environment in order to output music for its user. The current functional configuration which involves the use of the speakers influences the shared context by changing the audio level in the environment. An alternative functional configuration could be the use of plugged-in headphones. The use of headphones allows the

3.2. Application Coordination

music application to continue the provision of its functionality. However, due to the use of headphones, the interaction with the context changes.

An uncoordinated adaptation of one or more applications may however not suffice to solve the problem of interferences. Up to the present, applications are not aware of other applications and their interaction with the shared context. Without the knowledge of dependencies of other applications, an application may iterate through its possible functional configurations to find an interference-free configuration. Considering the previous example, the music application could try to adapt itself changing the output devices it uses. Since it is not aware of the fact that the reason of the interference is the changed audio volume, the adaptation is a trial and error process. Depending on the number of possible configurations this process may be highly inefficient. Moreover, the goal of solving an interference may not be achieved if the adaptation of a single application does not suffice but requires the adaptation of multiple applications. Consequently, a coordinated application adaptation is needed for an effective and efficient interference resolution.

The goal of this thesis is the development and realization of an approach to coordinate applications in pervasive systems in terms of interference detection and their resolution. The approach must be tailored to the specific characteristics discussed in Section 3.1. These characteristics can be summarized into three facts: firstly, pervasive systems are heterogeneous; secondly, pervasive systems can be highly dynamic; thirdly, pervasive systems are open with respect to new uni-platform pervasive systems.

With regard to heterogeneity, this is true not only for the system software employed, but the concept (smart environment vs. smart peer group), provided functionality, and used application model. With regard to dynamism, this is a function of user mobility: new users and/or devices may be brought into (or be removed from) a pervasive system, thereby adding a new user to an existing subsystem or a new uni-platform pervasive system to the pervasive system. With regard to openness, the consequence of this is that the actual set of users, devices, pervasive applications, etc. is not known before runtime.

3.3. Requirements

Based on the previous discussion, requirements towards an approach for application coordination need to be derived. The functional requirements towards the framework are (1) the detection of interferences as the need for coordination and (2) the resolution of detected interferences realizing a coordination. In addition, the application coordination framework should fulfill a number of nonfunctional requirements (Requirement I through Requirement VIII) which are discussed in the following.

I. System Integration

The first requirement addresses the heterogeneity of pervasive systems. According to the system model, pervasive systems will be a composition of a number of different and heterogeneous pervasive subsystems. These systems are likely to differ with respect to a variety of aspects. They will employ different system software, may have different application models, configuration algorithms, and adaptation frameworks among a variety of other aspects. Likewise, the executed applications are heterogeneous. Consequently, the framework for application coordination should support the integration of arbitrary applications irrespective of their system-specifics. The approach should be independent of a particular application class or model. It should allow for applications to participate in application coordination which act autonomously or which are coordinated within a uni-platform pervasive subsystem. In summary, the system must be realized as a cross-system design which allows the integration of arbitrary applications in application coordination.

II. System Autonomy

The second requirement ties in with the previously discussed requirement. While the approach should aim at the integration of arbitrary and heterogeneous systems, system-specific characteristics should be preserved. Each pervasive subsystem must be able to use its own system software and to manage itself independently. Likewise, the specifics of the realization and execution of pervasive applications must be maintained. This includes the

3.3. Requirements

used application model, the adaptation framework, the realization of context-awareness etc. In summary, the approach should enable an integration without the need to significantly change existing systems. Each pervasive subsystem should remain autonomous while being integrated into application coordination.

III. Runtime Coordination

The third requirement addresses the characteristics of a pervasive system to be highly dynamic and open with respect to users and devices. An important implication of these characteristics is that the actual set of users and devices in a pervasive system at a certain point in time is hardly predictable. Consequently, the approach must coordinate applications in terms of interference detection and resolution at runtime. In the optimal case interferences should be handled before they actually occur. The achievement of this goal would provide a basis for real interference avoidance. However, due to the characteristics of the system, interference avoidance is unlikely to be achieved. Thus, the system must provide means to detect and resolve interferences when they actually occur.

IV. Application-Specific Interferences

The fourth requirement also addresses the characteristics of the system to be dynamic and open with respect to users and devices. Interferences are often subjective and are strongly dependent on a user or an application. Considering the scenario where music is playing in the same room while a user is talking on the phone. This situation may pose an interference for user Anne who feels disturbed by the music while talking on the phone. Another user who finds himself in the same situation may enjoy listening to music while talking on the phone and may not encounter this situation as an interference. Moreover, interferences are not necessarily mutual. The user who is playing the loud music does not necessarily perceive the parallel phone call as an interference. Consequently, the system should be able to detect application-specific interferences. It needs to know which interferences may occur dependent on the users and applications executed in the environment. Moreover, the system needs to be able to cope with the dynamism of the system. The set of users and applications may change over time leading to changes in the set of interferences which are likely to occur in the system.

Furthermore, an interference may involve more than two applications. A context which is produced by a single application may have an impact on a number of m applications. Turning on a light in an environment with multiple applications which rely on a dark light level may force the reaction of several applications in parallel. On the other hand, a complex context may be a product of multiple applications. Thus, a single interference may be caused by a number of n applications. Respectively, m applications may cause an interference for n applications as well. A system that detects and resolves interferences must be able to handle such $n : m$ interferences.

V. Minimal User Distraction

The approach should aim at automatic detection and resolution of interferences as far as it is possible. Obviously, many interferences can be perceived by users and can be solved on the user level through social mechanisms. However, pervasive systems aim at the assistance of users in their everyday tasks. The withdrawal of user attention from their primary task to handle an interference contradicts this goal. Consequently, the distraction of users should be avoided when it comes to interferences and application coordination should be done automatically.

VI. Strategy-Based Coordination

Once an interference has been detected it needs to be resolved in order to yield an interference-free system state. The resolution of an interference involves the adaptation of a selected set of applications. In order to choose these applications a number of different criteria can be used. However, the focus of this work is not to develop and realize a single specific resolution strategy but to provide a framework which is able to support arbitrary resolution strategies which can be set according to the needs of the pervasive system.

VII. Correctness of Interference Detection

The seventh requirement towards the approach to be taken is the correctness of interference detection. The characteristic of being correct states that interference detection reports interferences if and only if an interference exists. It neither detects an interference in an interference-free system nor leaves an interference undetected.

VIII. Completeness of Interference Resolution

The completeness of interference resolution states that the approach finds a resolution if a resolution to an interference exists. Furthermore, the interference resolution process terminates after finite amount of time with a result of the computation. The result is either a viable solution to the interference or the indication that no solution exists.

To summarize this chapter, the research goal for the thesis at hand was defined. For this purpose, the characteristics of the targeted pervasive systems were summarized in a system model. The targeted systems are dynamic, heterogeneous and open with respect to users, devices, and the pervasive applications which are executed at runtime. Subsequently, the idea of application coordination as the approach to handle interferences in pervasive systems was introduced. The need for application coordination was motivated and requirements towards the approach to tailor it to the target systems were identified and discussed.

4. Related Work

This chapter discusses related work with respect to interferences. Section 4.1 addresses the notion of interferences. It presents existing definitions or concepts which are similar to the concept of interferences. Subsequently, Section 4.2 analyzes approaches for application coordination. After an introduction of frameworks which address application coordination in pervasive systems, Section 4.2.1 and 4.2.2 discuss related research which focuses on interference detection and resolution.

4.1. Interference

The analysis of existing literature has shown that no research work exists which defines or addresses the problem of interferences in its generality. However, a number of approaches address subclasses of the defined problem under the terms *interferences*, *service interactions*, and *conflicts*. In [MD06] [MD07] Morla *et al.* define an interference as a situation where the behavior of a component in a deployed system differs from its behavior in isolation. The participants of an interference are usually two entities which are connected via the environment. An interference occurs when the first entity changes the environment which causes the second entity to behave differently as if in isolation. The authors distinguish between three different classes of interferences, *generative interference*, *destructive interference*, and *distortional interference* depending whether input from the environment has been added, removed, or modified. The authors give a brief overview of the framework which consists of a notation to describe interferences and a discussion of five generic resolution possibilities. These resolution possibilities are based around the modification or removal of one of the entities. Furthermore, they suggest the filtering of information made to the environment or being read from the environment.

The problem of interferences has also been addressed as the *service interaction problem* by [KMW03]. A service interaction happens between two services when services have different goals towards the state of the environment. The authors define four different kinds of service interactions namely the *multiple action interaction*, the *shared trigger interaction*, the *sequential action interaction*, and the *missed trigger interaction*. The first type of interaction refers to a situation where an exclusive service is requested to perform different operations. The last three types describe interactions which may occur through the use of a shared environment. As certain states of the environment serve as triggers for services and this state can be modified through other services, these types of service interactions may happen. A single environmental state may be a trigger for two or more services which perform conflicting actions. A missed trigger may happen if the environment is changed by another service such that the service is not triggered. Lastly, the sequential action interaction describes a chain of triggers. This happens when the environment triggers a service which in turn changes the environment triggering yet another service.

An intersection set with interferences are the *conflicts* which have been addressed in various research approaches such as [SHW05], [RC03], [PLH05], [CEM03], [LPP+07], [SLS05], [AKM06], [HME+06], [DIK02], [HAM+06], and [JCL11]. In summary, three different classes of conflicts can be identified. 1) The *resource conflict* ([SHW05], [OSWS06], [JCL11], [HME+06] [LPP+07]) describes a conflict in which two or more users access an exclusive service with conflicting goals. For example, the use of the TV for two different TV channels can be considered a resource conflict. 2) The second class of conflicts is the class of *service interference conflicts* ([SHW05], [SW09], [AKM06], [PLH05]). A service interference occurs if two services are executed in a way that their impacts on the environment interfere with each other. Services may be executed by one as well as by multiple users. A good example is the execution of a music service and a television service which both affect the environment with sound. If the sound is too loud the two services interfere with each other and the quality of their functionality decreases. 3) The third class of conflicts are the *intra-service conflicts* ([DIK02], [SLS05], [CEM03], [RC03]). An

4.1. Interference

intra-service conflict describes a situation in which a service or application cannot unambiguously determine how to react to a certain state of the environment. Often these types of conflicts occur in systems where the behavior of an application is rule- or policy-based using context information as a basis. While each single rule itself seems to be reasonable, for certain context states they may prove to be different. An example is when two people have specified contradicting preferences for the temperature in the room. If only one person is present, the system can unambiguously determine how to react. However, the fact that both people are in the room at the same time leads to an intra-service conflict.

As the prior discussion shows, a variety of concepts or definitions exist for the problem of interferences. None of the definitions covers exactly the problem of interferences as they are addressed in the context of this thesis. Morla et al. [MD06], for example, refer to an interference as a situation where the behavior of a ubiquitous component in a multi-user/multi-application environment differs from that in isolation. In contrast to this, we assume that applications actually work as intended as they have been designed to react to context changes and adapt respectively. However, the fact that context may be produced by applications and consequently applications directly influence each other via the common context they share is the problem which was identified. A similar problem where the behavior of components – here services – in multi-service environments differs from that in isolation has been referred to as service interaction problem by Kolberg et al. [KMW03]. However, services in this system model do not represent the interests of different users. In contrast, it is the interest of the system that all services function correctly and work together in the way that each service can be provided correctly.

In the research area of conflicts the notion of service interference conflicts covers a subset of interferences as they are defined in the context of this thesis. They cover the part where the influences of two or more applications interfere with each other such that the quality of the provided functionality decreases. The situation in which the context influences of one application force another application to adapt are not covered by this concept.

4.2. Application Coordination

The analysis of existing work showed that subclasses of interferences have been identified and addressed under the terms interference, service interaction, and conflict. Approaches exist which propose frameworks to solve the problem of coordination in terms of interference detection and resolution in pervasive systems ([BRK06], [Bor06], [BCRZ09], [SRL10], [MD06]).

The group of Bortenschlager *et al.* ([BRK06], [Bor06], [BCRZ09]) has taken first steps to approach the problem of application coordination in pervasive systems. In [Bor06] and [BCRZ09] the authors analyze requirements of pervasive systems and present the UbiCoMo infrastructure for agent-based/application-based coordination in such environments. Furthermore, they introduce a number of patterns as a theoretical basis to model situations which require coordination and to handle them [BRK06]. Another general approach for the detection and resolution of interferences is introduced by Morla *et al.* [MD06]. They present a general framework that allows for the detection and analysis of interferences in pervasive systems and provides solutions to solve them.

Silva *et al.* [SRL10] address conflicts that arise in collective ubiquitous context-aware systems. The basic assumption of their work is that services in a ubiquitous environment can be shared by several users. Conflicts in this setting occur if multiple users require the service to adapt differently depending on their individual user profiles. Conflicts are detected over three input dimensions, namely application tasks, user profiles, and environment characteristics. Each user is required to provide an action level file defining the user's requirements towards these dimensions. A conflict is detected if the union of all action level files leads to an inconsistent system state. In order to solve conflicts, the approach introduces a conciliation module which provides several conflict resolution algorithms. The task of conflict resolution is the task of adapting the application according to the users' interests. At runtime the module selects an algorithm considering the specific characteristics of the conflict as well as energy requirements aiming at the adaptation of the service with the greatest user satisfaction.

4.2. Application Coordination

The works of Bortenschlager et al. ([BRK06], [Bor06], [BCRZ09]) and Morla et al. [MD06] provide a general approach for coordination and interference management in pervasive systems. In contrast to the framework presented in this thesis, the considerations remain on a theoretical level. The infrastructure and the patterns provide a basis for coordination in pervasive systems. However, a coordination at runtime and its challenges is not addressed. Likewise, Morla et al. have analyzed in detail how interferences can occur in pervasive systems and how they can be resolved in general. They propose a framework to model entities in pervasive systems in an abstract manner and enable developers to reason about their behavior in isolation and in combination with further entities. The research work however aims at providing developers with a system that supports interference management offline and is not applicable at runtime.

While the approach of Silva et al. [SRL10] suggests to be closely related to the one presented in this thesis, their definition of conflicts differs significantly from the one given in this thesis. According to Silva et al. conflicts occur when multiple users have different requirements towards a single service. Thus, the task of conflict resolution involves the adaptation of the single service aiming at the highest possible overall user satisfaction. In contrast, this thesis addresses interferences involving multiple applications in a shared context. Consequently, the resolution of an interference involves the adaptation of a set of applications with different configurations instead of a single one.

In contrast to the discussed research work which aims at frameworks to manage interferences (conflicts) in pervasive systems, further approaches exist which mainly focus on specific aspects of interference detection and resolution. Section 4.2.1 discusses approaches which realize interference detection. Approaches which are summarized in Section 4.2.2 neglect the process of interference detection and exclusively focus on the development of resolution strategies.

4.2.1. Interference Detection

The detection of interferences, service interactions, and conflicts has been the focus of a number of research projects ([KMW03], [PLH05], [SW09], [AKM06], [SLS05], [LPP$^+$07],

[DIK02], [JCL11]). In order to detect interferences the majority of these approaches rely on a model of a pervasive environment. This model typically comprises applications, services, resources, and environmental variables and a specification of their possible relationships ([PLH05], [SW09], [KMW03], [AKM06], [JCL11], [MAJ07]). At runtime these models are instantiated with real-time objects such as resources which are currently available in the pervasive environment or devices which are used and how they affect environmental variables. For interference detection the approaches define a set of patterns which describe interferences (conflicts) in terms of specific model structures. An interference is detected in an instantiated model if such a pattern is found at runtime.

As an example, Shin and Woo [SW09] have developed an ontology to model smart home environments. In addition to static information such as devices and resources which are permanent parts of the smart home, instance data is required at runtime and thus has been added to the ontology. Conflicts in the smart home environment occur if multiple applications share properties, share resources or share conditions. To detect conflicts the authors have defined three patterns covering the identified situations. At runtime, the ontology is frequently checked for the occurrence of these patterns indicating the existence of a conflict.

Another example is the approach by Kolberg *et al.* [KMW03]. The authors present a static model for the smart home domain. The model consists of three layers, the *service layer* which comprises the services in the home, the *device layer* consisting of all devices in the environment and the *environmental layer* which represents the state of the physical environment in form of environmental variables. Connections between entities of the layers are made if for example a service uses a certain device or when the use of a device has an effect on an environmental variable. In addition, three different kinds of access attributes have been introduced which are set by services during runtime. Using an access attribute services can state whether or not the use of a device can be shared. Analogously, it can be stated if an environmental variable may exclusively be influenced by a specific device or if several devices may set the variable and increase or decrease its value. A conflict occurs and is detected in two different scenarios: 1) If a service requests the use

4.2. Application Coordination

of a device which has been marked exclusive by another service. 2) If a device requests to change the value of an environmental variable which is marked exclusive or wants to increase/decrease a value that's marked as decrease-only/increase-only.

Other approaches which focus on interference detection do not require a model of the entire pervasive system but opt for using a collection of all potential conflicts that may occur in the system or a collection of all conflict-free states respectively ([LPP+07], [DIK02], [SLS05]). Lee *et al.* [LPP+07] for example propose a lock-based approach in order to detect conflicts in pervasive systems. The basic idea of the approach is to require applications to request a lock at a central component in order to make use of a resource. The central component then checks if granting the lock will yield a conflict-free system state. For this purpose, it employs a database which contains entries about all possible conflict-free lock combinations which need to be defined by an administrator before runtime. A similar approach is taken by Dunlop *et al.* [DIK02]. Conflict detection relies on a database of possible conflicts which have been identified before runtime. In order to detect conflicts, the current situation is compared to the scenarios specified in the database.

The discussion of related work shows that a number of approaches exist which realize interference (conflict, service interaction) detection in pervasive systems. These approaches can be split into two categories. The first category uses models and patterns that describe interferences as a certain structure within a model. Interferences are detected at runtime by searching for the patterns in the model which is instantiated with objects of the pervasive system. This approach models interferences independent of specific instances and thus enables a general applicability. In contrast, the second category of approaches employs a collection of specific situations which have been identified as interference/interference-free. In order to detect an interference the actual state of the environment is compared to the situations specified in the collection.

Compared with the approach presented in this thesis none of the existing approaches is able to handle application-/user-specific interferences. The use of patterns to detect interferences as well as of a collection of system states that pose/do not pose an interference does not take the subjectivity of interferences into account. A specific structure in the model or a specific pre-defined situation is considered to be an interference for an application independent of its user's perception. Likewise, very specific context states which may in general not be considered as interference but may be perceived as an interference by a specific user cannot be handled either. As an example, consider the previously mentioned situation when a phone call arrives while music is playing in the environment. The described situation may pose an interference for one user while another one likes to listen to music while talking on the phone. However, the discussed approaches cannot assess whether or not this situation is an interference for specific user.

Moreover, the discussed approaches which make use of a collection of interfering/interference-free system states do not take the openness and dynamism of the environment into account. The discussed approaches assume that the collection grows over time leading to a comprehensive description of interfering system states. However, as interferences depend on users and applications in the pervasive system, these approaches lack the ability to adapt accordingly and to cope with the dynamism. In contrast to that, the approach presented in this thesis considers the openness and dynamism of the targeted pervasive systems through a dynamic set of interference specifications.

4.2.2. Interference Resolution

A variety of research work exists which addresses the problem of interference (conflict, service interaction) resolution in pervasive systems ([LPP+07], [HME+06], [JCL11], [RC03], [KMW03], [SW05], [CSW05], [SYW07], [SDW08], [SW09], [MD06], [OSWS06], [SHW05], [PLH05], [TJK+08], [MAJ07], [SRL10]). The majority of these approaches focus on the development of one specific resolution strategy.

For example, the use of priorities to solve a detected conflict has widely been investigated ([LPP+07], [HME+06], [JCL11], [RC03], [KMW03], [SW05], [CSW05], [WKM07], [SLS05], [MAJ07]). Especially in scenarios where conflicts occur due to multiple access on exclusive resources, a priority-based resolution strategy has shown to be successful. Haya et al. [HME+06], for example, approach the resolution of concurrent requests to

4.2. Application Coordination

exclusive resources by employing preemptive priority queues. A centralized mechanism is used to store action requests on resources in queues. Each action request has a pre-defined priority. If several requests for a resource exist in a queue, the request with the highest priority is chosen. A similar approach is taken by Kolberg *et al.* [KMW03] for the service interaction problem. Each service in the home environment is assigned a priority. If two or more services try to use a device which is marked as exclusive, the access is granted to the service with the higher priority. Priority-based resolution strategies are also employed for interferences (conflicts) that occur between different users. Shin *et al.* [SW05] and [CSW05] dynamically assign priorities to users based on their context conflict history. If a user's context is likely to lead to a conflict according to the history, the user is assigned a low priority. A dynamic priority assignment is also proposed by Masoumzadeh *et al.* [MAJ07]. In the presented approach policies are used to define which activities are allowed and prohibited in a pervasive system. A conflict occurs if contradicting policies are detected within one system. To solve the conflict the authors present an algorithm which dynamically computes priorities for the conflicting policies enabling a decision. Likewise, Syukur *et al.* [SLS05] define a priority order for users in the environment or spaces in general. If a conflict occurs between the owner of a pervasive environment and a visitor for example, the owner is granted the execution of the service while the service of the visitor may not be executed. Another area of applicability for a priority-based resolution process in presented by Ranganathan *et al.* [RC03]. In the presented approach priorities are used to solve intra-service conflicts. An intra-service conflict occurs if the service has different choices considering the reaction to a given context. Consequently, the approach assigns priorities for context-action rules of applications. In case more than one context-action rule is applicable for a given context the one with the highest priority is chosen.

Further approaches that can be found in the literature are those that resolve conflicts based on user preferences ([SHW05], [PLH05], [TJK+08]). These approaches are based on the idea that users have preferences towards services and how they are composed, e.g. use of specific resources. An interference (conflict) occurs if a service is accessed by multiple users or when multiple services share limited resources. The resolution of a detected conflict is achieved by computing service compositions trying to optimize user satisfaction based on preferences.

The previously mentioned approaches provide a single strategy to automatically resolve interferences (conflicts). None of them require interaction with the user during the resolution process. In contrast to this, approaches exist which combine several resolution strategies and require the interaction with the user. For example, Shin et al. ([OSWS06], [SYW07], [SDW08], [SW09]) have developed a process that provides three resolution strategies and determines which resolution strategy is suitable for a resolution depending on the characteristics of a detected conflict. The first two strategies support an automatic resolution of a conflict. They make use of user preferences or assign priorities to users respectively. The third strategy is referred to as technology augmented social mediation and requires the interaction with the user. Technology augmented social mediation works on the basis of user preferences. The central idea of this approach is that in case of a conflict a centralized device compiles a list of service recommendations based on the group of users and their preferences. The list is presented to each user on their devices and users are prompted to make a selection. The approach then decides whether the group can agree on a specific service and selects the service respectively.

The discussed approaches can be distinguished between approaches that aim at the provision of a single resolution strategy and approaches that integrate a resolution strategy selection process. In contrast to these approaches, the focus of this thesis is the support of arbitrary resolution strategies instead of one explicit one. Those strategies can be based on priorities or preferences or may as well analyze the characteristics of a detected interference and automatically choose a resolution strategy. They can be implemented by a developer and can be set for a specific environment respectively. Moreover, some approaches differ significantly from the one presented in this thesis due to their definition of interferences/conflicts. Syukur et al. [SLS05] and Ranganathan et al. [RCAM+05], for example, address conflicts that occur when an application cannot unambiguously determine how to adapt in a certain context state. In this situation, a conflict resolution

4.2. Application Coordination

involves to determine which action needs to be chosen for a single application. However, a coordinated adaptation of several applications is not addressed.

In summary, the discussion of related work showed that no approach exists which handles the problem of interferences in its entirety as addressed by this thesis. A variety of research work exists which focuses on the management of subsets and intersection sets of the interference problem. Other approaches focus on the development of specific resolution strategies assuming a prior detection. The only approaches which present comprehensive frameworks for interferences remain on a theoretical level and are not applicable to practical pervasive systems.

5. Framework for Application Coordination

This chapter presents the theoretical approach to application coordination in pervasive systems. A framework is introduced that detects interferences between pervasive applications and resolves them through a coordinated application adaptation. Section 5.1 discusses the major design decisions for the taken approach. Subsequently, Section 5.2 introduces the framework, presents its compositional parts and explains the mode of operation. Section 5.3 then discusses how applications of different systems are integrated into application coordination and describes the required system extensions. Finally, Section 5.4 gives an in-depth analysis and presentation of the tasks of interference detection and interference resolution and discusses its underlying theory in detail.

5.1. Design Rationale

In order to handle interferences in multi-platform pervasive systems, a framework for application coordination has been developed in the context of this thesis. The framework is able to detect interferences across different uni-platform pervasive systems and to resolve them respectively. The following subsections – 5.1.1, 5.1.2, and 5.1.3 – discuss the three major design decisions for the framework, namely the design as a cross-system coordination layer, the extension of existing application systems and the realization of strategy-based application coordination. The design decisions were made in dependence on the requirements identified in Section 3.3. They tailor the approach to the multi-platform pervasive systems described in Section 3.1.

5.1.1. Cross-System Coordination Layer

The first major design decision is to realize the application coordination framework as a cross-system layer approach as shown in Figure 5.1. It has been designed to span across an arbitrary number of uni-platform pervasive systems, while it is also employable within one system only. The layer coordinates the interaction of pervasive applications in different uni-platform pervasive systems with the shared context.

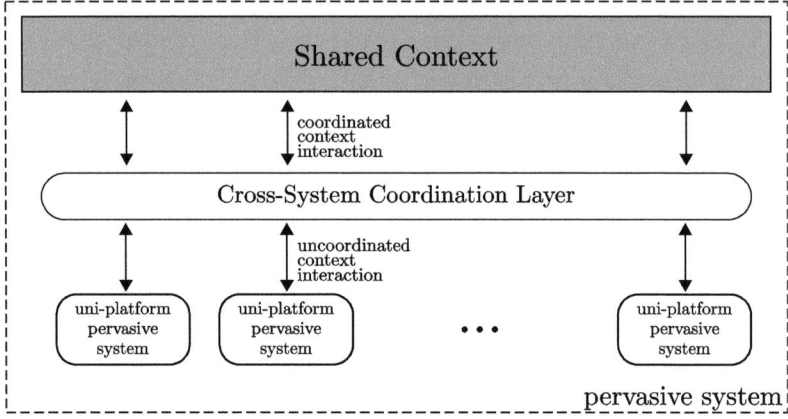

Figure 5.1.: Cross-System Coordination Layer

The coordination is based on the idea that each application provides the framework with information about its context interaction. This comprises how the application depends on the context and how it influences the context in its execution. The knowledge about current context interaction of all pervasive applications in the system enables the framework to detect interferences and thus the need for coordination.

In order to resolve the interference, the framework requires knowledge about the application's context interaction in possible alternative functional configurations. Based on the set of all alternative context interactions, the framework can compute how applications must reconfigure and thus change their context interactions. To implement the resolution, the framework initiates application adaptations according to the computation results. For

5.1. Design Rationale

this purpose, it requires the ability to request an application to switch to an alternative functional configuration.

The design of the coordination framework as a cross-system layer satisfies Requirement I and III, namely system integration and coordination at runtime. With respect to system integration, the framework requires knowledge about context interactions for the current and alternative functional configurations and the application's ability to instantiate a requested configuration. Besides these requirements application systems are treated as black boxes. The framework does not require an application system to use a specific application model or adaptation framework. It abstracts from system-specific characteristics and thus enables the integration of applications in arbitrary pervasive subsystems into application coordination.

Since an application's context interaction serves as a basis, interference detection and resolution must be realized at runtime. The context interaction of an application as well as the set of active applications is hardly predictable before runtime. The provision of this information as well as application reconfigurations at runtime satisfy the requirement for runtime coordination.

5.1.2. Extension of Existing Application Systems

The second design decision is the extension of existing application systems to enable the framework to coordinate applications. As described in the previous section, each application system needs to realize certain functionalities. At first, each application needs to provide information about its context interaction in its current and all alternative functional configurations. Secondly, each application system must enable the framework to instruct its applications to switch to a selected alternative functional configuration. The functionalities have been defined such that they can be realized as extensions to already existing functionalities of existing pervasive applications. Each extension should be implemented in accordance to the specifics of the respective application system.

The realization of information about the context interaction is achieved by extending the functional configuration by a *context configuration*. The context configuration adds two new sets of data to an application's overall configuration namely the *interference specification* and the *context influences*. The interference specification explicitly specifies all possible context states which the application considers as interferences. Up to the present, this information is only known to the application itself. Since applications are context-aware, the context changes which require an application reaction can be inferred from the rules that define an application's context-awareness. Furthermore, pervasive systems may employ user preferences to provide the application with more information regarding user goals and satisfaction. Based on this information, for example, interference specifications can be composed. The context influences in turn explicitly specify which impact an application has on the shared context when being executed. They depend on the resources which are employed in an application configuration and the actuators an application makes use of. In order to provide this information, the effects of the use of resources and actuators on the shared context need to be explicitly specified. In contrast to the information required by interference specifications, this information is not yet accessible by pervasive applications. To retrieve this information two steps are necessary. Firstly, each resource and actuator needs to be provided with information about how they affect the environment when being used by an application. Secondly, applications must be extended in the way that they are able to retrieve this information and to pass it on to the framework as part of the context configuration.

In addition to the realization of context configurations, existing systems are extended to determine a set of alternative context configurations and to be able to instantiate a certain configuration on request. As discussed in the system model 3.1, the ability to compute alternative functional configurations is assumed for pervasive applications. The extension involves that each pervasive application is also able to compute the context configuration of the alternative configuration and provides this information to the framework. In addition, pervasive applications are extended in the sense that they are able to instantiate a specific configuration if the framework requests it. Up to the present, the decision which configuration to initiate and when an adaptation happens is exclusively

5.1. Design Rationale

made by the application. The extensions allow the framework to request the instantiation of a specific configuration for application coordination purposes.

The extensions of existing systems, as they are described above, satisfy Requirements II and IV, viz. preserving system autonomy and handling application-specific interferences. The way existing systems are extended allows arbitrary applications to participate in application coordination while preserving their system specifics and autonomy. Since the extensions need to be done for every system, they can be realized in compliance with the used application model, the adaptation framework etc. The discussed changes do not interfere with the way a specific pervasive subsystem is managed. The extension of the application configuration requires the explicit specification and collection of context-related information. The way applications are built and executed as well as all major system services remain the same. At last, the introduction of interference specifications satisfies the requirement to handle application-specific interferences. Interference specifications always depend on a specific user or application. They allow the definition of those context states that an application, and thus a user represented by its application, considers as an interference. By providing an interference specification, the application is ensured that the framework monitors the pervasive systems for the specified interferences and takes measures to solve them.

5.1.3. Strategy-Based Application Coordination

The third major design decision is the realization of a strategy-based application coordination. As Section 5.4.2 discusses in detail, the process to resolve an interference consists of two steps. The first step involves the determination of which and how applications must reconfigure themselves in order to resolve an existing interference. An application reconfiguration, however, can be costly [BMV10]. Based on the assumption that an application uses the best possible configuration in the current system, a reconfiguration may lead to the instantiation of a viable but suboptimal configuration. Furthermore, due to the reconfiguration, delays in the service provision may happen. Thus, the the set of applications as well as their alternative configurations can be selected along a variety of different criteria and may also be influenced by the environment. As an example, in an office environment it might be reasonable to assign rights and priorities to users in the system. A team manager might have more rights than a regular team member who in turn may have more rights than business partners who come to visit the company once in a while. If an interference occurs between applications of users with different rights, a resolution might pick the application with less rights for an adaptation.

To allow the use of different resolution criteria, the framework supports the use of interchangeable resolution strategies. The development and use of a specific coordination strategy may however require additional information which may either be managed within the framework or which needs to be provided by participating applications. With respect to the example of using rights and priorities for users, the framework needs to be aware of this information when computing a resolution plan. A conceivable realization could be a provision of a user database which allows the framework to retrieve the rights and priorities of users and applications. Another possibility is to enable applications to provide the respective information. For example, the use of preferences and utility values for configurations obviously requires applications to provide the respective information.

The design decision aims at the satisfaction of Requirement V and VI, i.e. minimal user distraction and support of exchangeable coordination strategies. The minimal user distraction highly depends on the resolution strategy that is employed. While interferences are automatically detected, a resolution strategy may be designed to require user interaction. However, if the strategy is able to resolve interferences without further user input, the user will not be distracted. As discussed, the integration of resolution strategies which use different criteria is possible in general.

The three major design decisions, the extension of existing systems, the design of the application coordination framework as a cross-system layer, and the strategy-based application coordination on demand satisfy Requirements I through VI which have been identified to realize an approach to application coordination in the targeted pervasive systems. In the subsequent section, the general approach for a framework for application coordination is presented. The discussion introduces the theoretical foundation of the framework. Actual runtime behavior – such as the deployment of components to devices and the points in time when data needs to be exchanged – are addressed in Chapter 6.

5.2. Framework Overview

The goal of application coordination is to allow for the unobstructed and parallel provision of functionality by multiple applications in multi-platform pervasive systems. Since the unobstructed provision of functionality can be impaired by interferences, interferences need to be managed. For this purpose, a framework for application coordination has been developed in the context of this thesis. The framework detects and resolves interferences for pervasive applications in multi-platform pervasive systems. The following discussion introduces the components of the framework, gives an overview of its mode of operation and describes how applications are integrated and coordinated at runtime. An overview and details of the framework have been published by the author of this thesis [MSS[+]10].

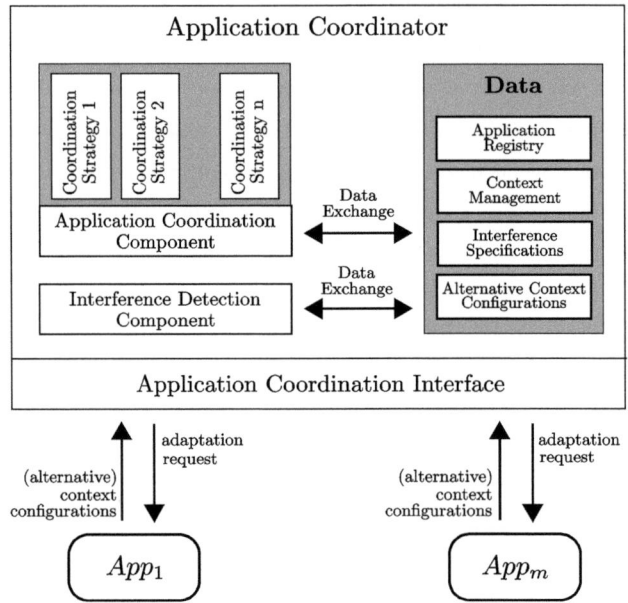

Figure 5.2.: Overview: Application Coordination Framework

5.2. Framework Overview

Figure 5.2 shows the overview of the *application coordination framework*, i.e. the application coordinator. It gives a detailed view on the application coordination approach depicted in Figure 5.1. The application coordinator realizes the cross-system coordination layer shown in Figure 5.1. It is responsible for the detection of interferences in a pervasive system and their resolution through a coordinated adaptation of applications. Each application App_i may belong to a different uni-platform pervasive system. In order to realize interference detection and resolution, applications are required to provide *context configurations* to the framework. A context configuration describes the interaction of the application with the shared context and depends on the application's functional configuration. It consists of the application's *interference specification* and its *context influences*. The interference specification enables an application to explicitly define the context states which pose interferences for the application. The context influences specify how the application influences the shared context.

The context configurations that need to be provided to the framework are subdivided into two types, the *active context configuration* and the set of *alternative context configurations*. The active context configuration is required for interference detection. It specifies the interaction with the shared context in the application's current functional configuration. A finite set of alternative context configurations is needed by the framework for interference resolution. Each alternative context configuration is linked to an application's alternative functional configuration. An alternative functional configuration is a configuration the application is able to instantiate in the given system. Consequently, an alternative context configuration specifies the expected interaction of the application in an alternative functional configuration. The provision of the context configuration as well as the alternative context configurations is realized at runtime using the *framework interface*. The interface offers all methods which are essential to subscribe and unsubscribe applications from application coordination and to allow them to provide and update the required data.

The coordination framework itself comprises several data and task components. With respect to the data components, the framework maintains an *application registry*, a con-

text management, a collection of *interference specifications*, and a set of *alternative context configurations*. The application registry maintains information about which applications have registered for application coordination. It allows context influences and interference specifications to be associated with a specific application and stores application callbacks to contact them in case of interferences. The context management maintains information about the shared context in the pervasive system. It provides the framework with the current state of the shared context and enables the framework to add context influences as context information to the system. The context which is held by the context management system may be fed by a variety of different sources. Physical sensors which are present in the pervasive system can capture and report the state of the physical environment to the context management system. The integration of information provided by virtual sensors which retrieve context information from online resources such as social networks is conceivable. Furthermore, high level context can be inferred from existing context information. The existence of different context providers – physical sensors, virtual sensors, inference engine – is neither assumed nor required but their integration is conceivable. Adding context information to the context management system however requires its association with at least one source. The source can be an application, a sensor, or a combination of sources for inferred context. The association with a context source is required to enable the framework to identify the applications which are involved in an interference. The third data set is the collection of interference specifications. The collection comprises all interference specifications of active context configurations which have been communicated to the framework. Thus, it holds all potential interferences which may occur in the pervasive system and for which the pervasive system is monitored. The last set of data is the set of alternative context configurations provided by all applications in the environment. Alternative context configurations are required by the framework for interference resolution. The set comprises all possible alternative context configurations of active applications.

The four data sets, as shown in Figure 5.2, provide the basis for the tasks of interference detection and interference resolution through a coordinated application adaptation. The

5.2. Framework Overview

tasks of interference detection and interference resolution are realized by the *interference detection component* and the *application coordination component* respectively. The task of the interference detection component is to monitor the pervasive systems for interferences. The existence of an interference indicates the need for coordination. For this purpose, the interference detection component relies on the data provided by the application registry, the context management, and the set of interference specifications. In the detection process it continuously evaluates every interference specification for the current context. An interference is detected if the context satisfies an interference specification. Consequently, the interference detection composes a description of the interference. The description includes the satisfied interference specification, the context which has led to its satisfaction and a list of all involved applications. Once the description has been composed, the interference resolution process is triggered by invoking the *application coordination component*.

The task of the application coordination component consist of two parts, the computation of an interference resolution plan and its realization through the initiation of application adaptations. The interference resolution plan is computed according to a coordination strategy which has been set for the pervasive system by an administrator. The coordination strategy determines how applications and the configurations they must initiate are selected. For the computation of the interference resolution plan the application coordination component relies on data provided by the set of alternative application configurations, the set of interference specifications and the context management. To find a resolution for an interference, the application coordination component needs to determine how applications must adapt to yield an interference-free system state.

Once an interference resolution plan has been computed, the application coordination component initiates the adaptations of the selected applications. The initiation is a simple request which is sent to an application to instantiate an alternative functional configuration which is linked to the selected context configuration. As the selected alternative context configurations have been computed by the pervasive applications themselves, their

```
interface Instructable {

    void adaptToCC(ContextConfiguration cc);

}
```

Figure 5.3.: Interface: Instructable

instantiation does not pose any additional challenges. As soon as applications receive the adaptation requests, the adaptations are performed and the interference is resolved.

5.3. System Extensions

The integration of pervasive applications requires the extension of existing application systems. The first extension is the realization and provision of context configurations. A context configuration defines an application's interaction with the shared context and provides the basis for interference detection and resolution. The computation and provision of context configurations constitutes the first part of an application's cooperation. If an application is not cooperative, i.e. not willing to determine and provide context configurations, its coordination is not possible.

The second extension enables the framework to request applications to initiate a specific configuration if required. To realize the second extensions, the *adaptation interface* `Instructable` shown in Figure 5.3 is introduced.

The interface has a single method – `adaptToCC` – which needs to be realized by pervasive application systems. It provides the framework with the ability to instruct an application to switch into an alternative functional configuration. As a parameter, the framework provides the context configuration the framework has determined to be interference-free. The functionality that needs to be realized by the application is its ability to instantiate a functional configuration that complies with the context configuration. If multiple functional configurations comply with the context configuration, the application may choose a suitable one. The realization of the adaptation interface constitutes the second part of

5.3. System Extensions 65

the application's cooperation. If the framework instructs an application to switch to an alternative functional configuration, the application must fulfill this task.

The ability to instantiate a matching functional configuration is based on the assumption that pervasive applications are able to compute alternative functional configurations as described in Section 3.1. Provided with the ability to determine context configurations in general, the computation of alternative context configurations is likewise possible. In order to fulfill the framework's request, the application selects a functional configuration which matches the context configuration requested by the framework. In this process, the application chooses from the functional configurations it has previously computed and which served as the basis to provide alternative context configurations to the framework.

5.3.1. Context Configuration

This section introduces the concept of a context configuration as one of the system extensions required for application coordination. A *context configuration* defines how a pervasive application interacts with the shared context. It depends on the functional configuration of an application, i.e. the resources and actuators the application uses.

For application coordination, the framework requires two different types of context configurations, an *active context configuration* and a list of *alternative context configurations*. The active context configuration specifies the interaction with the shared context in the application's current functional configuration. It is required by the framework for interference detection. An alternative context configurations specifies the expected interaction of the application in an alternative functional configuration. The provision of a list of alternative context configurations is needed by the framework for interference resolution.

In the following, the components of the context configuration are discussed in detail. A major challenge for the realization of context configurations is to ensure that the shared context is addressed by all pervasive applications in a common way. For this purpose, an ontology is introduced in Section 5.3.1.1 and a definition of an ontology is given. Based on this, the concepts of interference specifications and context influences are defined and presented in Sections 5.3.1.2 and 5.3.1.3 respectively.

5.3.1.1. Context Ontology and Context

A common addressing of the shared context is a prerequisite to enable an application coordination by the coordination framework. As pervasive applications are context-aware per definition, they are likely to use and have access to context information that is specific to their own system. To maintain system autonomy, the decision was made that applications are only required to address context in a common way which is required for application coordination. The management and use of context information that is exclusive to a uni-platform pervasive system is expected to coexist.

In order to provide a common understanding and the possibility to address the shared context, the definition of a common vocabulary for the shared context is required. The specification of a vocabulary for a shared domain is called an *ontology* [Gru93]. An ontology is a model for a distinct part of the real world. It consists of types, properties and relationships which map to the concepts of the real world. According to Gruber [Gru93] ontologies are used as a commitment for applications to allow a communication about a domain. An application commits to an ontology if its actions are describable with the concepts defined by the ontology.

For application coordination the use of an ontology serves two purposes. At first, it provides a model of the physical environment which represents the shared context for applications in pervasive systems. It defines the structure of the model, its elements and the possible values the elements may have. Secondly, it defines the elements which can be used by applications to specify their interactions with the context. This involves the creation of interference specifications and context influences which compose the context configurations. The formal definition of a context ontology of a pervasive system is given by Definition 2.

Definition 2 (Context Ontology)
The context ontology defines a model for the shared context of pervasive applications in a pervasive system. The context ontology CO is a set of:
1) properties and
2) object types and their properties.

5.3. System Extensions

A **property** has the form:

$$p = (name, \{(value\_type_1, value\_range_1, \{relop_1^1, \ldots, relop_r^1\}) \ldots,$$
$$(value\_type_n, value\_range_n, \{relop_1^n, \ldots, relop_s^n\})\}).$$

An **object type** has the form:

$$t = (name, \{property_1, \ldots, property_n\}).$$

A property models a characteristic of the physical environment. It defines its possible value types, the valid value ranges and the supported relational operators used by interference specifications. An object type models objects of the physical environment and their characteristics using properties.

The ontology defines the properties which characterize the physical environment. These properties represent attributes such as the temperature, the humidity, or the light level of the physical space. The object types in the ontology are used to model objects and their attributes within the physical space. A typical example for an object type is a user, who is characterized by her name, gender, or date of birth. In addition to the property and object types, the ontology defines restrictions in the sense of valid value types and value ranges. Furthermore, it specifies the relational operators which can be used. If an application commits to an ontology, its interference specifications and context influences need to be in accordance with the vocabulary and restrictions of the ontology.

In order to keep the considerations in this chapter on a general level, the specific ontology is presented as part of the implementation in Chapter 7. For the subsequent discussion, the knowledge about the structural elements of the ontology suffices. Given an ontology, a context state can be defined as follows:

Definition 3 (Context State)

Let $CO = \{p_1, \ldots, p_n, t_1, \ldots, t_m\}$ be a context ontology. A context state is a set:

$CTX_{CO} = \{\ p_1 = value_1, \ldots, p_n = value_n,$

$$t_1.p_1 = value_1^1, \ldots, t_1.p_m = value_m^1,$$
$$\ldots$$
$$t_j.p_1 = value_1^j, \ldots, t_j.p_o = value_o^j\}$$

where $value_i$ and $value_k^i$ are the values of property p_i and type property t_k^i respectively, in compliance with the ontology CO.

According to the definition, the context is an instance of the ontology which represents the current state of the physical environment. Each property as well as each type property is assigned a distinct value in compliance with the restrictions of the ontology. Having defined the context ontology and the context, the subsequent section introduces the interference specification as the first part of the context configuration.

5.3.1.2. Interference Specifications

The interference specification is the first part of an application's context configuration. It enables a pervasive application to define context states which pose interferences for the application. Being provided with an interference specification, the coordination framework ensures that the specified interferences will be detected and measures will be taken to resolve them.

Interference specifications play a crucial role in the processes of interference detection and resolution. Thus, their nature has a strong impact on the complexity and efficiency of the entire application coordination process. In order to reason about the complexity, a formal model for interference specifications needs to be selected. The selection process must consider two aspects. The first aspect is the expressiveness of the model. In the ideal case, an interference specification should support the specification of arbitrary context states. To start with, simple statements over the value of context variables such as environmental attributes are needed. As an example, an application may specify an interference if the light level in the environment is set to anything but dark or if the noise level is above a certain value. As a next step, simple statements should be combinable in order to specify more complex system states. An application could define an interference

5.3. System Extensions

if the combination of both – a bright light level and the noise level above a certain value – happens at the same time. In addition to combined simple statements, the specification of the existence of certain objects such as persons or devices may be needed. The user could define an interference in the situation when a phone call arrives while being in the same room with user Bob. Furthermore, it can be desirable to make statements about characteristics of a set of entities in the environment and relationships between them. The existence of a group of people who are all part of the same team is as an example.

The second aspect that needs to be considered for the selection of a formal model is the efficiency with which expressions are evaluated. Interference specifications are used by the framework for the task of interference detection and in the process of computing an interference resolution. For interference detection, the framework evaluates every interference specification for each context change. The evaluation of interference specifications is a continuous process which only pauses if the environment remains static. With respect to the computation of an interference resolution plan, interference specifications also play a crucial role. The task of computing an interference resolution plan consists of finding alternative configurations for applications such that the current context does not satisfy any interference specification. A reconfiguration of an application however may imply the change of context influences and interference specifications. Consequently, the framework needs to evaluate the changed set of interference specifications for the changed context. The details of computing an interference resolution plan and its complexity are discussed in depth in Section 5.4.2.1.

Another situation in which the evaluation of interference specifications proves to be reasonable is a consistency check for its set. Each interference specification constrains the possibilities of interference-free interactions of other applications within the shared context. Thus, the collection of interference specifications specifies the system states with interferences. Any system state that is not modeled in an interference specification is interference-free.

The framework aims at maintaining an interference-free system state. If an interference occurs it takes measures to resolve the interference yielding an interference-free pervasive system. Problems however occur if the collection of interference specifications constrains the use of the shared context in a way that every system state poses an interference. Consider the example where two applications add an interference specification to the framework. The first application specifies a bright light level as an interference. The second application specifies a light level that is everything but bright as an interference. The combination of the two interference specifications constrain the modification of the light level in the sense that every possible light level results in an interference. To overcome this problem it is conceivable to check if the combination of interference specifications leaves possibilities for interference-free system states. For this purpose, the satisfiability of the set of interference specifications needs to be computed.

The expressiveness of a model and the efficiency with which model-based expressions are evaluated have a strong influence on each other. With increasing expressiveness of a formal model, the efficiency of expression evaluation decreases. In order to select a formal model for interference specifications, the tradeoff between expressiveness and efficiency needs to be considered.

A variety of different logics exist which can provide a formal model for interference specifications. However, instead of giving a comprehensive overview of existing logics and a thorough analysis of their characteristics, three candidate logics, namely *propositional logic*, *monadic first-order logic* and *first-order predicate logic* have been selected. The logics have been chosen as they cover the possible space of formal models that can be used as theoretical foundation for interference specifications. While propositional logic proves to be very strong with respect to expression evaluation it is limited considering its expressiveness. First-order predicate logic in comparison is far more expressive than propositional logic but has drawbacks when it comes to the efficiency of expression evaluation. Monadic first-order logic is situated in the middle between propositional and first-order predicate logic expressiveness-wise and with respect to the efficiency of expression evaluation.

Table 5.1 gives an overview of the expressive power of the three logics. From the three logics, propositional logic is the least expressive one. It allows simple and negated state-

5.3. System Extensions

Aspects/Logic	Prop. Logic	Monadic FO Logic	FO Predicate Logic
Simple Statements	X	X	X
Neg/Comb. Statements	X	X	X
Exists/Forall	-	X	X
Predicates	-	arity 0-1	arity 0-n
Functions	-	-	arity 0-n

Table 5.1.: Overview: Logic Expressiveness

ments to be made and to combine the simple statements into more complex expressions. With respect to the shared context this allows statements to be made about the light level and the temperature of the environment or a combination of both. Monadic first-order logic and first-order predicate logic extend propositional logic by universal and existential quantifiers. Quantifiers allow statements to be made about a set of entities or to specify the existence of an object. In addition to quantifiers, monadic first-order logic as well as first-order predicate logic provide the use of predicates. A predicate represents a function that evaluates to the truth value *true* or *false*. A predicate often relates to elements in a set of objects and is used to make statements about the property of an object. For interference specifications the use of quantifiers in combination with predicates enables an application to specify the existence of a person with a certain name, for example, or to state that a group of people works in the same company.

As the table shows, monadic first-order logic allows for the use of predicates of arity zero and one. First-order predicate logic in contrast supports the use of predicates of arbitrary arity. Using a predicate of an arity greater than one allows to model relationship between elements. A typical example is to specify that a person is the boss of another person. The last aspect of the discussed logics are functions. The use of functions is only provided by first-order predicate logic. Functions evaluate to objects in the world. While propositional logic and monadic first-order logic do not support the use of functions, first-order predicate logic does. With respect to interference specifications the use of functions allows to deduce further objects such as the boss of person with name Bob.

The previous discussion reveals that propositional logic as a formal model for interference specifications is not suitable. Especially the use of quantifiers and predicates which address elements in sets and allow for statements to be made about them, provides an expressiveness that is desirable for interference specifications. Considering monadic first-order logic, predicates are restricted to arities of null and one. Thus, the modeling of arbitrary relationships – even of binary relationships – is not possible using monadic first-order logic while this is supported by first-order predicate logic. As previously mentioned, first-order predicate logic provides interference specifications with the greatest expressiveness. However, the expressiveness has a strong impact on the efficiency with which expressions in a specific logic are evaluated.

Table 5.2 gives an overview of the complexity of statement evaluation – the evaluation of an interference specification – and the computation of satisfiability – the consistency check for newly added rules. In order to provide the entries in the table with proper semantics, let φ be a formula in the respective logic and $|\varphi|$ the number of variables in the formula. Furthermore, let $\mathcal{A} = (\mathcal{U_A}, \mathcal{I_A})$ be a structure where $\mathcal{U_A}$ is the universe of $\mathcal{A}$ and $\mathcal{I_A}$ is an interpretation function that assigns 1) each n-ary predicate symbol P an n-ary predicate symbol over $\mathcal{U_A}$, 2) each n-ary function symbol f an n-ary function symbol over $\mathcal{U_A}$, and 3) each variable x an element from the universe $\mathcal{U_A}$. Moreover, let $|\mathcal{A}|$ be the number of elements in the structure. Then, the complexity for expression evaluation can be defined as given in the first row of Table 5.2.

Aspects/Logic	Prop. Logic	Monadic FO Logic	FO Predicate Logic
Expression evaluation	$O(|\varphi|)$	$O(|\varphi||\mathcal{A}|)$	$O(|\varphi||A|^{|\varphi|})$
Satisfiability	decidable	decidable	undecidable

Table 5.2.: Overview: Logic Complexity

The entries in the table show that the complexity of expression evaluation increases with the expressiveness of the logic. While propositional formulas can be evaluated in a straightforward manner, monadic first-order logic requires additional effort due to the treatment of sets. In contrast to the former two logics, the evaluation of formulas in

5.3. System Extensions

predicate first-order logic is far more complex due to the existence of relationships and functions of arbitrary arity.

The second aspect that needs to be considered is the determination of satisfiability of expressions to perform consistency checks on the set of interference specifications. As the table shows, the satisfiability problem in propositional logic as well as in monadic first-order logic is decidable and NP-complete as it has been shown by Cook [Coo71] and Löwenheim [Löw31]. The characteristic of being decidable means that an automated process exists which can solve the problem. The satisfiability problem in first-order predicate logic in contrast is undecidable as shown by Church [Chu36]. Thus, there exists no general effective procedure that can solve the problem.

In summary, considering the tradeoff between the expressiveness and the evaluation efficiency of statements, monadic predicate logic has been selected as the formal model for interference specifications. The discussion has shown that the use of propositional logic proves to be efficient with respect to expression evaluation but lacks required expressiveness. First-order predicate logic in contrast provides a strong expressiveness but proves to be inefficient with respect to expression evaluation. Moreover, the fact that the satisfiability of expressions in propositional logic is undecidable makes the logic inapplicable for consistency checks. Compared to propositional logic and first-order predicate logic, monadic predicate logic resides in the middle of the two logics. It provides a greater expressiveness than propositional logic while still allowing for an efficient expression evaluation. Furthermore, the logic is decidable with respect to the computation of satisfiability. The formal definition of interference specifications based on monadic first-order logic is given in Definition 4.

Definition 4 (Interference Specification (IS))

Let $CO = \{p_1, \ldots, p_n, t_1, \ldots, t_m\}$ be a context ontology with:

$p_i = (name^i, \{(value\_type_1^i, value\_range_1^i, \{relop_1^{i1}, \ldots, relop_{s_1}^{i1}\}) \ldots ,$
$\qquad (value\_type_o^i, value\_range_o^i, \{relop_1^{io}, \ldots, relop_{s_o}^{io}\})\})$ and

$t_j = (name^j, \{p_1^j, \ldots, p_p^j\})$ with

$$p_l^j = (name_l^j, \{(value\_type_1^{jl}, value\_range_1^{jl}, \{relop_1^{jl1}, \ldots, relop_{t_1}^{jl1}\}) \ldots,$$
$$(value\_type_q^{jl}, value\_range_q^{jl}, \{relop_1^{jlq}, \ldots, relop_{t_q}^{jlq}\})\}).$$

A unary **predicate** P_{CO} according to the ontology CO is defined as:

1. $name^i \; relop_a^{il}$

   with $i \in \{1, \ldots, n\}$, $l \in \{1, \ldots, o\}$, and $a \in \{1, \ldots, s_l\}$ for properties.

2. $name^j.name_l^j \; relop_b^{jlr}$

   with $j \in \{1, \ldots, m\}$, $r \in \{1, \ldots, q\}$, and $b \in \{1, \ldots, t_l\}$ for object properties.

An interference specification is built as follows:

1. If P is a predicate and x is a variable then $P(x)$ is an **atomic context constraint**.

2. If ACC is an atomic context constraint then $\neg ACC$ is an atomic context constraint.

3. If x is a variable and ACC is an atomic context constraint then $\exists x ACC$ and $\forall x ACC$ are atomic context constraints.

4. If $ACC_1, \ldots, ACC_i$ with $i = 1, 2, 3, \ldots$ are atomic context constraints then $ACC_1 \wedge \ldots \wedge ACC_i$ is a **composed context constraint**.

5. If $CCC_1, \ldots, CCC_i$ with $i = 1, 2, 3, \ldots$ are composed context constraints then $CCC_1 \vee \ldots \vee CCC_i$ is an **interference specification (IS)**.

To ease the discussion throughout this thesis, a set-based notation for interference specifications is used as follows:
$IS = \{CCC_1, \ldots, CCC_n\}$
where $\{CCC_1, \ldots, CCC_n\}$ denotes $CCC_1 \vee \ldots \vee CCC_n$ and
CCC_i has the form $CCC_i = \{ACC_1^i, \ldots, ACC_{m_i}^i\}$
where $\{ACC_1, \ldots, ACC_{m_i}\}$ denotes $ACC_1 \wedge \ldots \wedge ACC_{m_i}$.

According to the definition, an interference specification is a disjunction of a set of conjunctions of atomic context constraints. The predicates which can be used depend on the properties and objects defined by the context ontology. The following is an example of an interference specification for a meeting application:

5.3. System Extensions

$IS = \{\ \{activity = meeting,\ audio.type = phone\}, \{\neg light.level = bright\}\}$

The interference specification consists of two composed context constraints. The first context constraint comprises two atomic context constraints according to which an interference occurs if a meeting takes place and the phone is ringing. The second constraint describes an interference when the light level is set to anything but bright. Note, that the interference specification is not defined for a specific environment. Once it is added to the application coordinator, the interference specification is valid for the physical space the coordinator is responsible for. Another example of an interference specification is the following:

$IS = \{\{audio.intensity = loud\}, \{\neg temperature\ inRange(18, 22, celsius)\}\}$

The interference specification could be defined for public spaces by an administrator of an office building. The interference specification is composed of two context constraints. The first constraint specifies that an interference exists if the audio intensity will be loud. The second constraint defines a temperature range. In case the temperature will be lower than 18 °C or higher than 22 °C, an interference occurs and measures will be taken to resolve it.

In order to be used by applications, interference specifications need to be defined by the application developer. A basic set of interference specifications can be derived from the rules that describe how an application adapts to a certain context. The derivation of these rules covers all interferences where another application forces the application to react. Furthermore, it is conceivable that a user adds further constraints to an application's interference specification. As an example, a user could define a high noise level to be an interference while listening to music. The high noise level does not necessarily must be covered by the application's adaptation rules. It is a user preference which is also specific to the individual user.

5.3.1.3. Context Influences

Context influences are the second part of an application's context configuration. They explicitly specify the effects an application has on the shared context in its execution. The context influences depend on the functional configuration of an application. They are determined through the resources and actuators an application uses.

Context influences are provided to the framework as part of an application's active context configuration and as part of each alternative context configuration. Within an active configuration context influences specify the actual impact of the application on the shared context in compliance with the used context ontology. Context influences of an application are added as context to the context management system by the framework. Definition 5 gives a formal description of context influences.

Definition 5 (Context Influences (CI))

Let $CO = \{p_1, \ldots, p_n, t_1, \ldots, t_m\}$ be a context ontology. A *single* context influence *has the form:*

1) $p_i.name_i := value_i$; *in compliance with the ontology* CO

   if a property p_i *is addressed or*

2) $t_i.name.p_j^i.name := value_j^i$; *in compliance with the ontology* CO

   if a property p_j *of the object* t_i *is addressed*

Context influences *are a collection of single context influences and are denoted by* $CI = \{ci_1, \ldots, ci_n\}$.

Note that the definition uses a JAVA-like notation to address the name of a property and types and their properties respectively. The expression *.name* is a function that realizes the retrieval of the name of the element. The following is an example for context influences which have been specified by a relaxing music application. The example also shows the result of the *.name* function.

$CI = \{$ $person.forename := Bob, activity := relax, light.intensity := dark,$

$audio.type := music, audio.intensity := 60dB\}$

5.3. System Extensions

The context influences state that a person with forename Bob is present in the environment. Furthermore, the context is influenced in the way that the activity of the environment is set to relaxing, the light intensity of the environment is set to dark and music is played with an intensity of 60dB.

While the context influences of an active functional configuration can be determined, the exact context influences of an alternative functional configuration are hard to predict. As a result, an alternative context configuration can only specify expected context influences as described formally in Definition 6.

Definition 6 (Expected Context Influences)
Let $CO = \{p_1, \ldots, p_n, t_1, \ldots, t_m\}$ *be a context ontology. A single **expected context influence** has the form:*

1) $p_i.name\ inRange\ (value^i_{min}, value^i_{max})$; *in compliance with the ontology* CO *if a property* p_i *is addressed or*

2) $t_i.name.p^i_j.name\ inRange(value^i_{j_{min}}, value^i_{j_{max}})$; *in compliance with the ontology* CO *if a property* p_j *of the object* t_i *is addressed.*

Expected context influences *are a collection of single expected context influences and are denoted by* $ECI = \{eci_1, \ldots, eci_n\}$.

To realize the specification of expected context influences the use of value ranges is supported. Once the configuration is instantiated, the actual value is communicated as part of the active context configuration. As an example, a navigation application that uses a visual representation could specify an audio-based navigation as alternative configuration. As the audio-based configuration is not instantiated yet it would specify the influence of the audio level in the environment between 50 and 80 decibel. Once the configuration is instantiated the actual value of 55 decibel is communicated as part of the active context configuration to the framework.

In addition to the fact that the actual value may not be known before a configuration is instantiated, the specification of a range of values also minimizes the number of alternative context configurations an application must provide. Instead of having to specify an alternative context configuration for each decibel value, the set of alternative context configurations which only differ in the decibel value can be summarized into a single context configuration.

5.4. Application Coordination Framework

The extensions of existing systems by context configurations enable the coordination of applications by the application coordination framework to manage interferences. In the following sections, the main tasks of the framework, namely interference detection and application coordination are discussed in detail.

5.4.1. Interference Detection

The first task of application coordination is the detection of interferences. Interference detection is realized by the interference detection component of the framework. The basis for interference detection is the set of interference specifications and the current context which is held in the context management system. The task of interference detection is to evaluate active interference specifications for the current context. The interference detection process is required when an interference specification is added to the coordination framework or when the context changes. In the former case, the interference detection process only needs to evaluate the new interference specification. In the case of a context change, all interference specifications must be evaluated for the changed context.

The reasons for a context change are twofold. Firstly, the context may change due to the effects of an application on the shared environment such as the use of a light switch. Secondly, the context may change due to a natural event such as the sunset which changes the light level. While interferences are caused by application-induced context changes per definition, triggering interference detection for natural context changes also proves to be reasonable. At first, a natural event may contribute to the occurrence of an interference. In that case, the interference can possibly be resolved by adapting those applications which contributed to the interference. Secondly, it allows an application to determine whether or not a context change can be ascribed to another application or to a natural

5.4. Application Coordination Framework

event. If the context change can be ascribed to a natural event, the application can react as it has been designed to do. Moreover, the framework can help the application to find a configuration that does not lead to an interference if desired.

Algorithm 1: *InterferenceDetection*

Input: IS : *Set of interference specifications*, CTX : *Context*
Output: *interferenceExists*

1 **begin**
2   for $IS^i \in IS$ do
3   for $CCC_j \in IS^i$ do
4   *interferenceExists* $\leftarrow$ *true*
5   *exists* $\leftarrow$ *false*
6   for $ACC_j^k \in CCC_j$ **and while** *interferenceExists* do
7   ACC_j^k **has pattern:** $(\neg)P(x)$
8   *interferenceExists* $\leftarrow$ $(\neg)satisfies(CTX, ACC_j^k)$
9   ACC_j^k **has pattern:** $\forall x P(x)$
10   for $ctx_x \in CTX$ do
11   if $satisfies(ctx_x, ACC_j^k)$ then
12   *interferenceExists* $\leftarrow$ *false*
13   ACC_j^k **has pattern:** $\exists x P(x)$
14   for $ctx_x \in CTX$ do
15   if $satisfies(ctx_x, ACC_j^k)$ then
16   *exists* $\leftarrow$ *true*
17   *interferenceExists* $\leftarrow$ *exists*
18   if *interferenceExists* then
19   **return true**
20
21   **return false**

Algorithm 1 describes the process of interference detection. In the process every active interference specification maintained by the coordination framework is evaluated for the current context. As discussed in Section 5.3.1.2, interference specifications are modeled based on monadic predicate logic. Recall that an interference specification is a disjunction of composed context constraints (CCC) which themselves are conjunctions of atomic context constraints (ACC). Consequently, the algorithm stepwise breaks down the interference specifications into atomic context constraints and evaluates them for the current context.

The presented algorithm follows a brute-force approach. It evaluates every interference specification in the set of interference specifications. However, for performance reasons optimizations are conceivable. The optimized version is presented and discussed in more detail as part of the prototype which is described in Chapter 7.

An interference is detected if an interference specification evaluates to true. Before the interference is handed to the application coordination component, a description of the interference is composed. The interference description comprises the satisfied interference, the context which satisfies the interference specification associated with the context sources, i.e. the interfering pervasive applications. The interference description serves as a basis for interference resolution as it provides all information relevant to the interference and its contributors.

The interference description is obtained through a small modification and extension of Algorithm 1. The algorithm needs to be modified in the sense that an interference specification is completely evaluated before a result is returned. In the presented version, the algorithm returns *true* as soon as a composed context constraint proves to be satisfied. As a consequence, subsequent composed context constraints are not evaluated. For the creation of an interference description however, the entire interference specification needs to be evaluated as its contents serve as a basis for interference resolution. The extension that is required is that the algorithm keeps track of the sources of a context that contribute to the satisfaction of the interference. If in line 8 for example, the context CTX satisfies ACC_j^k, the algorithm needs to retrieve the context source of CTX and add it to the description.

As described in Section 3.1, a requirement towards interference detection is Requirement VII, the correctness of interference detection. A process is said to be correct if it returns a correct output for a given input. In the context of application coordination, interference detection is correct if it reports an interference if one exists and does not report an interference if no interference exists.

In the framework, interference detection is the truth evaluation of expressions in monadic predicate logic. The truth evaluation of monadic predicate logic is known to be correct.

5.4. Application Coordination Framework

Thus, the correctness of interference detection strongly depends on the quality of the context model. The quality of a context model states how accurate the digital representation of the real world matches the actual physical. If the context model is an exact digital copy of the real physical world then interference detection is correct. The interference detection process will eventually detect an interference if one exists and will report those interferences only.

However, in practice the context model is unlikely to be an exact digital image of the real world. One of the reasons is that the context information that is captured by sensors and fed into the context model may not be 100 % accurate. Furthermore, several context reporting resources may exist for the same context variable and are likely to report different values. The temperature in a room may for example differ slightly close to the window in comparison to the entrance door. Furthermore, the context influences of applications need to be processed as well in order to obtain unambiguous context information. With the variety of context information and its uncertainty, an exact digital representation of the real world is hardly obtainable.

5.4.2. Interference Resolution

The second task of application coordination is the interference resolution. The resolution of a detected interference is realized through a coordinated application adaptation. The coordinated application adaptation is the task of the application coordination component of the coordination framework. The application coordination component is invoked as soon as an interference description has been created by the interference detection component. The basic idea to resolve a detected interference is a coordinated adaptation of applications.

The task of interference resolution is split into two subtasks: 1) The computation of an interference resolution plan and 2) the instruction of applications to adapt according to the plan. The second step is realized through a call on the interface, applications must implement, as described in Section 5.3. The adaptation request includes the context configuration which has been selected for the application as a result of the interference resolution plan computation. It initiates the application to instantiate the functional configuration which belongs to the context configuration. The computation of an interference resolution plan, in contrast, is a complex task. The following sections discuss the theory of the problem in general and its implications on the process to solve the problem.

5.4.2.1. Interference Resolution Plan Computation

An *interference resolution plan* is a list of active applications where each of these applications is assigned one context configuration. The realization of each application-specific assignment resolves the detected interference and yields an interference-free system state. An assignment can be one of three options: (1) no changes are required, (2) an adaptation is required, or (3) a pause is required. While the first two assignments allow the continuation of functionality provision, the request to pause an application does not. Whether or not pausing is considered as an option depends on the pervasive system and the desired coordination strategy.

In order to compute an interference resolution plan, the framework relies on the alternative context configurations which are provided by each application in the pervasive system. In the process, the framework searches for a context configuration for each application such that the detected interference is resolved and no new interferences are created. That means, an assignment needs to be found for each application such that (1) the context influences of the application combined with the current context do not lead to the satisfaction of any interference specification and (2) the interference specification of the application is not satisfied by the current context which also includes current context influences.

The complexity of the problem stems from the fact that context influences and interference specifications are strongly related with each other. The context influences on one hand change the context based on which interference specifications are evaluated. The interference specification on the other hand restricts the possible context influences. Changing the context configuration of an application is likely to change the context influences as well as the inference specification of the application. As a result, the instantiation

5.4. Application Coordination Framework

of an alternative context configuration may lead to the satisfaction of the new interference specification or to the satisfaction of an existing interference specification due to the new context influences.

Consider the following example of three pervasive applications (App_1, App_2, App_3) which are active in the same pervasive system. Table 5.3 shows the active context configuration in terms of interference specifications (IS) and context influences (CI) of each application. Furthermore, each application has one alternative context configuration and thus an alternative interference specification and alternative context influences. The example uses symbols as a placeholder for context variables and their values in order to provide a clear example.

Aspects/Logic	App_1	App_2	App_3
Active IS	$A \lor B$	$A \land C$	$D \lor E$
Active CI	B	A	E
Alternative IS	$A \lor C$	A	$\neg D$
Alternative CI	E	$B \land D$	$D \land B$

Table 5.3.: Example: Interference Resolution Problem

According to the active context configurations, the current context has the following state $CTX = \{A, B, E\}$ and the set of interference specifications $IS = \{A \lor B, A \land C, D \lor E\}$. The evaluation of the set of interference specifications for the current context result in the satisfaction of the interference specification of App_1 through the context influences of App_2. Consequently, an interference exists between the two applications. Note that applications cannot cause interferences for themselves, i.e., App_3 does not have an interference with itself.

In order to determine an interference resolution plan, the process needs to find assignments for each of the three applications. Going through the example, the process could try to adapt application App_1. However, assigning App_1 an alternative context configuration would cause a new interference between App_1 and App_3 as the alternative context influences of App_1 lead to the satisfaction of the interference specification of App_3. The same problem occurs if the process assigns the alternative context configuration exclusively to application App_2. In this case an interference would be caused between App_2 and App_3. The only viable solution in this scenario is the assignment of alternative context configurations to all three applications. The context that results from the reconfiguration of all App_1, App_2, and App_3 creates a context $CTX = \{B, D, E\}$ and a set of interference specifications $IS = \{A \vee C, A, \neg D\}$, yielding an interference-free system state.

The discussed example illustrates the interdependency between context influences and interference specifications. The single adaptations of App_1 or App_2 or the adaptation of both in combination solves the existing interference but leads to the creation of a new one involving application App_3. The example also shows that the adaptation of initially interfering applications does not necessarily suffice. The resolution of the initial interference and the transformation into an interference-free pervasive systems requires the integration of the uninvolved application App_3.

As stated at the beginning of this section, the framework can also assign the pausing of an application if required which is often the easiest way to solve an interference. In the example described above, pausing application App_2 for example would solve the existing interference. However, pausing an application implies that the application cannot provide its functionality anymore. Whether or not this is acceptable strongly depends on the environment of the pervasive system. In an office environment for example the automated ventilation may be paused if it disturbs participants of an important meeting. In contrast, if all active applications are of great importance pausing an application may not be an option.

Based on the previous discussion, the problem of the interference resolution plan computation is formalized as follows:

Definition 7 (Interference Resolution Plan Problem)
Let PS be a pervasive system and $App_1, ..., App_n$ active applications in PS. Furthermore, let $CC(App_i) = \{cc^i_{active}, cc^i_1, ..., cc^i_{m_i}, cc^i_{paused}\}$ be the set of context configurations of application App_i with $cc^i_j = (CI^i_j, IS^i_j)$ and cc^i_{active} being the active context configuration, $cc^i_1, ..., cc^i_{m_i}$ being the set of alternative context configurations and $cc^i_{paused} = (\{\}, \{\})$

5.4. Application Coordination Framework

being the context configuration when being paused. Furthermore, let CTX_{nat} be the current context which is produced by natural events. Thus, the interference resolution plan problem is defined as follows: For each application App_i find an assignment such that $\bigcup_{i=1}^{n} CI_j^i \cup CTX_{nat}(\bigcup_{i=1}^{n} IS_j^i) \models 0$, i.e., the resulting context does not satisfy the set of active interference specifications.

Finding a solution to the problem proves to be complex as the question of whether or not the context configuration of the k-th application is viable depends on applications $App_1, \ldots, App_{k-1}, App_{k+1}, \ldots, App_n$. Based on the assumption that each application App_i has at most m context configurations, $O(m^n)$ combinations need to be evaluated in order to find a solution if a solution exists at all.

5.4.2.2. Interference Resolution Plan Problem as CSP

In order to develop a suitable approach to compute an interference resolution plan, an analysis of the complexity of the problem needs to be made. The problem is obviously NP-complete. In order to show this, the problem of computing an interference resolution plan is modeled as a constraint satisfaction problem (CSP) [RN03]. Since CSPs have been shown to be NP-complete [Ben96] [Wal00], the NP-completeness of the interference resolution plan computation problem is shown. A constraint satisfaction problem is formally defined in Definition 8.

Definition 8 (Constraint Satisfaction Problem (CSP))
A constraint satisfaction problem is a triple (V, D, C) *where* $V = \{V_1, \ldots, V_n\}$ *is a finite set of variables and* $D = \{D(V_1), \ldots, D(V_n)\}$ *is a set of finite domains such that* $D(V_i)$ *is the finite set of potential values for* V_i. *Furthermore,* $C = \{C_1, \ldots, C_k\}$ *is a finite set of constraints where each* C_l *is a pair* (t_l, R_l) *with* $t_l = (v_{l_1}, \ldots, v_{l_m})$ *being an m-tuple of variables and* R_l *being an m-ary relation over* D.
*A **solution of an instance of a CSP** is a function* $f : V \to D$ *such that* $\forall (t_l, R_l)$ *with* $t_l = (v_{l_1}, \ldots, v_{l_m})$ $(f(v_{l_1}), \ldots, f(v_{l_m})) \in R_l$.

Given Definition 8, the problem of computing an interference resolution plan can be modeled as a constraint satisfaction problem as follows: Let V be the set of applications which are active in the environments $App = \{App_1, \ldots, App_n\}$ and let $Conf(App) = \{Conf(App_1), \ldots, Conf(App_n)\}$ with $Conf(App_i) = \{(CI_{i_1}, IS_{i_1}), \ldots, (CI_{i_m}, IS_{i_m})\}$ the finite domain of App_i, namely the finite set of possible configurations for App_i. Furthermore, let $C = (t, R)$ be the single constraint with $t = (App_1, \ldots, App_n)$ and $R = \bigcup_{i=1}^{n} CI_{i_j} \cup CTX_{nat}(\bigcup_{i=1}^{n} IS_{i_j}) \models 0$. Thus the solution to the computation of an interference resolution plan is a selection of a configuration for each application such that the union of the context influences of all applications in combination with the natural context (CTX_{nat}) does not satisfy the union of all interference specifications.

5.4.2.3. Algorithms for Constraint Satisfaction Problems

Having modeled the problem of computing an interference resolution plan as a constraint satisfaction problem, any algorithm that solves an instance of a constraint satisfaction problem can in general compute an interference resolution plan. A variety of different algorithms for solving CSPs exists which can be split into four different classes ([Kum92] [DF98]) namely *Backtracking, Constraint Propagation, Intelligent Backtracking and Truth Maintenance*, and *Local Search Algorithms*. In the following, a brief description of each class is given preceded by a discussion of their suitability for the targeted systems.

Backtracking: The basic *Backtracking* algorithm to solve constraint satisfaction problems was first introduced by Bitner and Reingold [BR75] even though the basic idea of backtracking can be traced back to the 19th century. Backtracking is a search method which uses a depth-first search. It chooses assignments for one variable at a time, successively finding a solution. If, in the process, the algorithm detects that no feasible value can be assigned for the i-th variable, it backtracks to the $(i-1)$-th variable, choosing a new value in order to continue with the procedure. Backtracking is complete which means that the algorithm eventually finds a solution to the instance of a constraint satisfaction problem if a solution exists. It is an uninformed search which systematically walks the

5.4. Application Coordination Framework

search space. In the worst case, the backtracking algorithm looks at every possible value combination resulting in an exponential runtime. Backtracking-based searches may however be improved using heuristics. The *most-constrained-variable* heuristic [BR75] which prioritizes the value assignment of those variables first which are constrained the most or the *least-constraining-value* heuristic [HE80] as the opposite are examples of domain-independent heuristics which have been employed to improve the search. Moreover, the use of heuristics which consider the structure of a specific CSP is also reasonable.

Constraint Propagation: One drawback of simple backtracking algorithms is the occurrence of thrashing [Gas79]. The term thrashing refers to the situation in which the value assignment of the i-th variable prevents a successful assignment for the k-th variable with $i < j < k$. This means that independently of which value the algorithm assigns for any variable between i and k, a solution cannot be found. In order to overcome this problem algorithms in the class of *Constraint Propagation* aim at keeping track which legal values remain for unassigned variables when assigning a variable. The goal of such algorithms is to transform the initial problem into a simpler one which can be solved more efficiently using backtracking but often also eliminates the need for backtracking at all [Wal75]. A concept which has been introduced in the context of constraint propagation is *arc-consistency*. Looking at the constraint graph of a constraint satisfaction problem, an arc between two variables (V_i, V_j) is said to be arc consistent if for every value x in the current domain of V_i there exists a value in the domain of V_j that is consistent with x. A number of algorithms such as AC-3 [Mac77], AC-4 [MH86], and MAC [SF94] exist which enforce arc-consistency on constraint graphs reducing the search space for a viable solution to the problem. Stronger approaches have been developed using the notion of k-*consistency*. A constraint graph is said to be k-consistent if for every value assignment for any set of $k-1$ variables, which is constraint-satisfying, there exists a value assignment for the k-th variable which is consistent. The constraint graph is said to be *strongly k-consistent* if it is i-consistent for all $i < k$. Through enforcing strong k-consistency the need for backtracking is eliminated. Algorithms exist which transform a constraint graph into a strongly k-consistent graph [Fre88] [Coo89]. The complexity of the search space reduction, however, is also exponential.

Intelligent Backtracking and Truth Maintenance: Basic backtracking is often also referred to as chronological backtracking as it always backtracks to the most recently assigned variable. The algorithm class of *Intelligent Backtracking and Truth Maintenance* modifies backtracking in the sense that it enables the algorithm to identify variables that cause a failure and to directly return to those in order to find a new assignment. *Conflict-directed backjumping* [Pro93], for example, maintains a so-called conflict set for every variable which is a set of previously assigned variables that are related to the variable via a constraint. In case the algorithm detects that no consistent value can be assigned to the current variable, the algorithm jumps back to the most recent variable in the conflict set in order to re-assign a new value. A more powerful and general approach to intelligent backtracking proved to be *dependency-directed backtracking* [SS77] which resulted in the development of *truth maintenance systems* [Doy79]. Truth maintenance systems are based on the idea that an algorithm chooses value assignments based on its beliefs. These beliefs are successively created throughout the process. Every time a variable is a assigned a value, the system justifies why exactly this value is assigned and saves the justification. In case a value is assigned which violates any constraint, a new node is created stating the inconsistency of the value combination. The created node again is used to justify another value assignment on the variable. The process is repeated until a consistent assignment for the variables, i.e., a solution to the CSP is found. The amount of search that such a system requires is minimal. However, the determination of the reasons of a failure and the selection of variables has proven to be complex and thus, the approach is often more costly than basic backtracking [CJP87].

Local Search: A last class of algorithms to solve instances of constraint satisfaction problems is *Local Search*. Local search algorithms are based on the idea of iterative improvement. An algorithm starts out with an initial assignment and improves the assignment locally in several iterations. The algorithm typically stops after a pre-defined

5.4. Application Coordination Framework

number of iterations or after a fixed period of time. Moreover, the algorithm may be developed to stop if a good enough solution could be found. In this case the algorithm requires an assessment function in order to determine the quality of a found solution. Iterative improvement typically uses a hill climbing [RN03] approach where an inconsistent value assignment is revised. A problem of hill climbing approaches is that an algorithm may get trapped in *local minima*. A local minimum is a state which is still inconsistent but it's not possible for the algorithm to decrease the number of violated constraints by re-assigning the value of a single variable. Approaches however exist which enable the escape from such local minima such as the *breakout* algorithm [Mor93]. Furthermore, heuristics exists which guide the selection of values for a variable. The *min-conflicts* [MJPL92] [Gu89] heuristic selects the value with the minimum number of conflicts it has with other variables and proved to be surprisingly effective for constraint satisfaction problems especially for the n-queens problem [SG94].

5.4.2.4. Discussion

In theory, any algorithm of the above discussed classes can be used to compute an interference resolution plan. As CSPs are NP-complete, none of the discussed algorithms outperforms another in general. However, depending on the specifics of the CSP in practice, some algorithms may perform better than others. The first algorithm discussed in the previous section is basic backtracking. In the context of computing an interference resolution plan, backtracking is a standard algorithm that systematically walks through all possible combinations. The algorithm terminates when it finds a solution or all combinations have been tested. The basic backtracking is a pure search algorithm. It walks the search space without considering the structure of the addressed problems – interferences in this situation – nor reducing the search space in the process.

Intelligent backtracking, in contrast, typically uses heuristics in order to improve the performance of the backtracking algorithm. With respect to computing an interference resolution plan, a heuristic could be used that exploits the structure of interferences. The algorithm could walk through those combinations at first that include the adaptation of interfering applications. In case the adaptation of interfering applications suffices to solve the interference, the heuristic is likely to improve the performance of the algorithm compared to an uninformed backtracking. However, if further applications need to be involved, an improvement might not be noticed.

Another possibility for intelligent backtracking is the reduction of the search space. The reduction of the search space is typically achieved through skipping combinations which are known to not provide a solution to the problem. In the context of interference resolution, intelligent backtracking could identify those application configurations that prevent a combination from being a solution to an interference. Without loss of generality, any combination that involves the identified configurations will not prove to be a solution to the interference. Given that knowledge, the algorithm is able to skip those combinations and to reduce the search space respectively. Such an algorithm promises to perform best for problems in which large parts of the solution space can be pruned.

In contrast to backtracking and intelligent backtracking, constraint propagation and truth maintenance systems spend more effort on the reduction of the search space to minimize the need for searching. Such systems suggests to be best suitable for pervasive systems which have a low dynamic and have a well-known set of users, applications, and their context configurations. In such a system, it seems to be reasonable to maintain a truth maintenance system or to propagate constraints and to adapt it respectively if the environment changes. This may significantly reduce the search effort.

In highly dynamic environments, the reduction of the search space may prove to be hardly applicable. Due to changes in the environment, the CSP is altered and the changes need to be considered in the truth maintenance system and for constraint propagation. If the changes impact the structure and contents of the truth maintenance system or the constraint propagation, the adaptation of the system may require a lot of effort. As a consequence, it might be more reasonable to spend effort in searching instead of reducing the search space, especially in dynamic environments.

5.4. Application Coordination Framework

Finally, algorithms in the class of local search also seem to be promising to compute an interference resolution plan in pervasive systems. In contrast to the previously discussed approaches, a variety of algorithms in this class exist which are not complete. The completeness is, however, a desired characteristic for the targeted systems as defined by Requirement VIII. Since interferences distract the users, they need to be resolved in order to maximize the potential of the pervasive system – the seamless provision of functionality. The completeness states that the algorithm finds a solution if one exists and otherwise reports that no solution can be found. The completeness guarantees that a resolution for an interference is found. Recall that pausing all applications solves the interference and is the fallback solution in case no combination of context configurations can be found.

5.4.2.5. Coordination Strategy Realization

In order to provide the framework with an actual coordination strategy, two intelligent backtracking approaches are presented in the following. Both algorithms are complete, which satisfies Requirement VIII. As discussed in the previous section, both algorithms use a heuristic which exploits the nature of interferences in order to improve the performance of the backtracking algorithm. In chapter 8, measurements are conducted which show how the used heuristics actually improve the backtracking-based search.

To provide a basis for the discussion on the heuristics, Algorithm 2 describes the process of computing an interference resolution using basic backtracking. As input, the algorithm takes a matrix of context configurations as shown in Figure 5.4. The x-axis of the matrix depicts the active applications $App_1, \ldots, App_n$ of the environment. The y-axis lists an application's context configurations, m at most. The matrix is designed in the way that the first row contains all active context configurations of the applications. All other rows contain alternative context configurations. The matrix shown in the figure has four applications which possess between three and five context configurations. A context configuration combination is a vector $com = (CC_{App1}, \ldots, CC_{Appn})$ where each application is assigned one of its context configurations. The connected nodes show a possible combination. The initial combination is $com = (1, 1, 1, \ldots, 1)$.

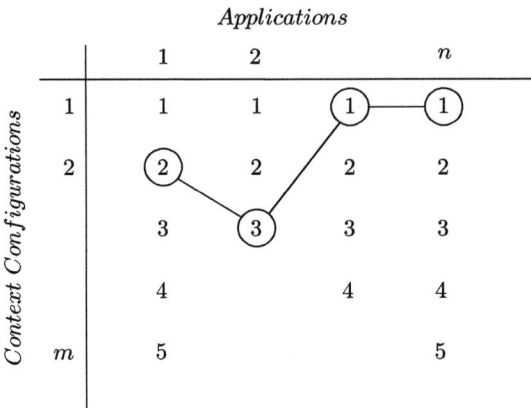

Figure 5.4.: Input Matrix of Applications and Context Configurations

---

Algorithm 2: *resolveInterference*

Input: *matrix : ContextConfigurationMatrix*
Output: *com : ContextConfigurationCombination*
1 **begin**
2   *com ← initialCombination(matrix)*
3   **while** *hasNextCombination(matrix, com)* **do**
4   *com ← nextCombination(matrix, com)*
5   **if** *isInterferenceFree(com)* **then**
6   **return** *com*
7   **return** ∅

Algorithm 2 realizes the computation of an interference resolution plan. The algorithm starts on the initial combination. The initial combination of context configurations is the one that represents the interference to be resolved. The algorithm then enters a loop. The loop is executed as long as the matrix of active applications and their context configurations hold another combination which has not been tested yet. Within the loop, the algorithm retrieves the next combination and checks it for interference-freedom. In case the combination proves to be interference-free, a solution has been found and the algorithm returns the respective combination. Otherwise, the algorithm remains within the loop until all combinations have been evaluated which also leads to its termination.

5.4. Application Coordination Framework

In the worst case, the algorithm checks all possible $O(m^n)$ combinations with n being the number of active applications and m being the maximum number of context configurations an application has.

The actual backtracking is realized in Algorithm 3. The algorithm systematically creates new combinations of context configurations. The algorithm takes the current combination *com* and the matrix of context configurations as input and starts with the last position of *com*. It checks if the application represented by the position possesses another context configuration. If this is the case, the new context configuration is selected and the algorithm returns a new combination. In case the application does not have any further context configurations, the first configuration of the application is selected. The algorithm then proceeds with the predecessor position. In case *com* already represents the last possible combination, the algorithm terminates indicating that no next combination could be found.

Algorithm 3: *nextCombination*

Input: *matrix*, $com = (CC_i, \ldots, CC_k)$
Output: p

1 **begin**
2   **for** $i = (length(com) - 1) \to 0 \in matrix$ **do**
3   **if** *(hasNextConfiguration(com[i]))* **then**
4              $com[i] \leftarrow getNextConfiguration(com[i])$
5   **return** p
6   **else**
7              $com[i] \leftarrow getFirstConfiguration(com[i])$
8   **return** NO_NEXT_COMBINATION

The combination of Algorithm 2 and Algorithm 3 realizes the computation of an interference resolution plan based on chronological backtracking. Starting with an initial assignment, the algorithm systematically creates new context configurations by adapting single applications. While the algorithm finds a solution if one exists, its performance can be improved by exploiting the structure of interferences.

ORDERING The first heuristic addresses the order for the selection of applications and their adaptations. The heuristic is based on the idea that those applications should be adapted at first which are actually involved in the interference that is to be resolved. Thus, the use of the ORDERING heuristic has an impact on how applications are sorted in the matrix.

To sort applications, the algorithm makes use of the information provided by the interference description which is created in the interference detection process. The interference description includes the satisfied interference specification, the context which is responsible for its satisfaction and the set of applications which produce the context. The processing of the interference description determines how often an application is involved in an interference. For example, if an application changes the activity of a pervasive system and has an impact on the audio volume and both influences contribute to an interference, its involvement in the interference can be counted as 2. An application that only influences audio volume which leads to the interference has an involvement of 1. Consequently, the application with the highest involvement is placed at the end of the matrix as its adaptation may already solve the interference.

The sorting of the matrix requires additional effort. In order to determine the ranking, the set of interference descriptions needs to be evaluated. In the worst case, each active context configuration interferes with each other resulting in $O(n)$ interferences. As a consequences, the complexity for matrix sorting is determined by the sorting algorithm itself, i.e., it is $O(n \cdot log(n))$.

PRUNING The basic idea of the second heuristic is that the algorithm skips combinations which involve sub parts that have proven to create an interference. Let $com = (CC_1, \ldots, CC_i, CC_{i+1}, \ldots, CC_n)$ be a combination of context configurations. If CC_1 and CC_i cause an interference, without loss of generality, no combination of $CC_{i+1} \ldots CC_n$ will lead to an interference-free state as the interference between CC_1 and CC_i will persist. This fact can be used in order to prevent the *resolveInterference* method to evaluate combinations by skipping those combination which is realized through pruning [RN03, p. 100]. Thus, the next viable combination which avoids the generation of combinations

5.4. Application Coordination Framework

with interferences can be obtained by CC_i and resetting $CC_{i+1}\ldots CC_n$. The process of pruning in the context of interference resolution is described in Algorithm 4.

Algorithm 4: *nextPrunedCombination*

Data: *matrix, com* $= (CC_i, \ldots, CC_k)$
Result: *com*
1 **begin**
2   **for** $i = (length(com) - 1) \to 0 \in matrix$ **do**
3   **if** *isInterfering(p[i])* $\wedge$ *hasNextConfiguration(p[i])* **then**
4   *com[i]* $\leftarrow$ *getNextPrunedConfiguration(com[i])*
5   **return** *com*
6   **else**
7   *com[i]* $\leftarrow$ *getFirstConfiguration(com[i])*
8   **return** NO_NEXT_COMBINATION

The use of pruning is realized by exchanging line 4 in Algorithm 2 with *com* $\leftarrow$ *nextPrunedCombination(matrix, com)*. The algorithm takes the matrix of active applications and their context configurations and the current combination. In this setting, the ORDERED heuristic is not used and applications are sorted in random order. The algorithm then searches for the first application – the ith application – that is involved in an interference starting with the nth application. Since the current combination holds the initial interference such an application will be found. If the ith application has further context configurations, the next context configuration for the ith application is selected. Furthermore, all applications $i+1^{st}$ to n^{th} are assigned their first context configuration. In the case that the ith application does not have any further context configurations, the algorithm proceeds with the $i+1^{st}$ application and assigns all applications i to n their first context configuration.

Figure 5.5 illustrates the results of the pruning process on the matrix. The current configuration in the figure is *com* $= (1, 3, 2, 1)$. A prior check for interferences has shown that the context configuration 1 of App_1 and context configuration 2 of App_3 create an interference – as indicated by the dotted circles. Consequently, the algorithm selects application App_3 as the first application to be involved in an interference starting from the end of the matrix. It then selects the next context configuration for App_3, preventing

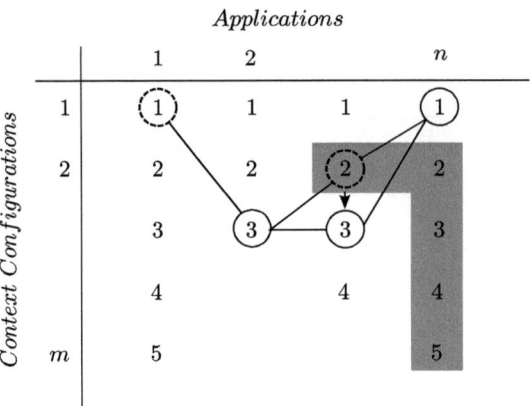

Figure 5.5.: Pruning Process

the evaluation of four combinations which will have proven to have an interference due to the context configurations of App_1 and App_3.

To conclude this chapter, the theoretical framework for application coordination was presented as the approach to manage interferences in pervasive systems. The three design rationales, cross-system coordination layer, extension of existing application systems, and strategy-based application coordination, make the approach unique and tailor it to the target systems. The required system extensions in form of context configurations and an adaptation interface were described in detail and a model for interferences was defined. Based on this model, the problem of interference detection was analyzed and a solution was presented. Furthermore, the problem of interference resolution plan computation was discussed in detail. An overview of algorithms to solve the problem was given and their applicability in dependence of pervasive system characteristics was discussed. Finally, a heuristic was presented that considers the specific structure of interferences to improve the process of interference resolution plan computation.

6. Application Coordination in Pervasive Systems

This chapter discusses the practical realization of the coordination framework for general pervasive systems. The realization comprises the deployment of task and data components as well as the definition of points in time when data must be exchanged. For this purpose, Section 6.1 discusses characteristics which have an impact on realization decisions. Section 6.2 then analyzes general pervasive systems with respect to these characteristics. Subsequently, Section 6.3 derives requirements towards a practical realization before the realization decisions for interference detection and resolution are presented in Section 6.4. The chapter concludes with a discussion on measures that need to be taken in dynamic pervasive systems in Section 6.5.

6.1. System Characteristics

The efficiency of application coordination in practical pervasive systems is influenced by two factors: (1) The placement of task and data components and (2) the points in time when required data is exchanged between remote devices. Depending on the characteristics of a pervasive system, decisions for component deployment and the point in time for required communication may differ. Two major factors which have an impact on these decisions are the *reliability* of devices in the system and their *resourcefulness*. Their implications on a practical realization are discussed in the following:

Reliability: The first characteristic which needs to be considered for a practical realization is the reliability of devices in the system. In the context of this thesis, a device is said to be *reliable* if it remains within the system throughout the entire system life cycle.

A reliable device is always reachable unless it becomes unavailable due to network or technical failures[1]. The existence of at least one reliable device enables the placement of data and task components on the device without the need to expect and cope with its sudden unavailability. This overcomes the need to maintain data backups or to support a dynamic reassignment of responsibilities. In contrast, pervasive systems without a reliable device need to be able to cope with an unpredictable unavailability of devices. If a device leaves the environment, data may get lost and the execution of assigned tasks may get interrupted. As a result, the practical realization needs to provide respective backup mechanisms if data and tasks cannot be assigned to a reliable device.

Resourcefulness: The second characteristic is the resourcefulness of devices in the system. In the context of this thesis a device is said to be *resourceful* if it is able to execute all tasks and maintain all data which is required for the realization of a specific functionality, i.e. application coordination. The existence of a resourceful device allows for the placement of task and data components without the consideration of available processing and storage capabilities. The device is not restricted with respect to the processing capabilities it uses nor its storage capabilities. The fact that the data storage is not limited also has an impact on the point in time when data must be exchanged. Due to non-restricted data storage, data can be pre-fetched and stored on the device. In contrast, resource-poor devices are limited with respect to their storage and processing capabilities. Thus, the amount of data as well as the need for processing capabilities needs to be minimized. The lack of resourceful devices can also have an impact on the point in time when data is exchanged. If a resource-poor device executes a task that requires access to remote data but lacks the required storage capabilities it needs to retrieve the data via the network during the process.

---

[1]The occurrence of technical failures is not explicitly covered in this thesis.

6.2. Smart Environments and Smart Peer Groups

Pervasive systems can be realized as smart environments, smart peer groups, or a combination of both, as discussed in Section 2.1. In the following, both approaches are analyzed with respect to their reliability and resourcefulness. The goal of the analysis is to derive characteristics for general pervasive systems. This allows a practical realization irrespective of whether the pervasive system uses a smart environment or smart peer group approach.

Smart Environment A smart environment is an infrastructure-based approach which is characterized by a predefined set of installed devices and the physical environments in which the devices reside. A smart environment can typically be considered to be resourceful. The infrastructure of a smart environment usually comprises at least one resourceful device such as a server or a personal computer. One of the resourceful devices is typically used to realize functionalities which are required to run the pervasive system such as a device registry, an application manager, or a context management system. It possesses enough capabilities to execute required tasks and to manage task-related data. For the same reason of having a fixed infrastructure, smart environments are considered to have reliable devices. As part of the fixed infrastructure, devices remain within the system throughout the entire system life cycle.

Smart Peer Group In contrast to smart environments, smart peer groups do not rely on a pre-defined infrastructure. A smart peer group is typically a spontaneously formed network of devices which are in communication range of each other. A smart peer group can be formed anywhere given the nearby devices are equipped with respective system software. Once a smart peer group has been established, the devices can directly communicate with each other and share functionalities on a peer-to-peer basis. As smart peer groups are spontaneously formed and may disband spontaneously just as well, their devices are considered to be unreliable.

A smart peer group is typically user-centric and moves with its user. As a result, new devices may be integrated into the smart peer group and devices may be removed as the user moves. Moreover, as the exact user movement is hard to predict, the set of devices may change unexpectedly. The characteristic of being user-centric also suggests that a smart peer group comprises at least one resourceful device. A user in the smart peer group is typically identified by a personal device such as a smart phone or a tablet pc. Nowadays, these devices possess enough processing and storage capabilities to perform the tasks of application coordination (cf. Section 8.1). Hence, smart peer groups can be assumed to comprise at least one powerful device at any given time.

General Pervasive Systems In summary, general pervasive systems can be assumed to contain at least one resourceful device. In a smart environment the resourceful device is part of the infrastructure. In a smart peer group the resourceful device is the personal device of the user.

The existence of a resourceful device has several advantages for the practical realization of application coordination. At first, a resourceful device enables the placement of the interference detection and the interference resolution component on a single device without the need to distribute the tasks among multiple devices. Secondly, a resourceful device allows for a local maintenance of the data required for application coordination without the need to explicitly limit its amount. Moreover, the unlimited storage capability allows pre-fetching of remotely available data and to maintain a local copy. The data copy can be used by locally-executed tasks, thus minimizing the need to retrieve data over the network in time-critical situations.

With respect to reliability, the existence of a reliable device cannot be assumed for pervasive systems in general. In a smart environment, a device which is part of the infrastructure can usually be considered to be reliable. In contrast, the reliability of a device cannot be assumed for smart peer groups. The unreliability poses challenges with respect to the execution of tasks and the availability of data. In smart environments, a reliable device can be selected for the assignment of tasks and the storage of data. Thus, the functionality will be provided throughout the entire life cycle of the system. However, the pervasive system may as well be realized as a smart peer group. Consequently, a mechanism is required to ensure the continuous provision of application coordination. In the case that the pervasive system uses a smart environment approach, the mechanism can be omitted.

6.3. Requirements

The discussion in the previous section has shown that general pervasive systems can be assumed to: 1) comprise at least one resourceful device and 2) not necessarily possess reliable devices. In order to tailor the practical realization of the theoretical application coordination framework to a general pervasive system, the realization must fulfill a number of requirements in addition to Requirements I through VIII:

IX. Coordination Efficiency

The first requirement towards a practical realization is the efficiency of the entire application coordination process. The process starts with a change in the context or the set of interference specifications and ends with the initiation of application adaptations. Since interferences are likely to disturb the user and pervasive computing aims at the unobstructed and seamless provision of functionalities, interferences should be detected and resolved as quickly as possible. In the ideal case, the user is not aware that an interference has been handled. Thus, the practical realization must aim at the minimization of the time required by the entire process.

X. Best-Effort Application Coordination

The second requirement towards a practical realization is to aim at a best effort application coordination. While in theory, interference detection is correct and accurate and interference resolution is complete, the characteristics cannot be guaranteed for practical pervasive systems. Interference detection, for example, is performed on the context model. If the context model does not hold an accurate representation of the real world, false positives and false negatives with respect to interferences are possible. Furthermore, it is conceivable that interferences are detected but disappear before they are resolved. Thus, application coordination should aim at best effort to keep the pervasive system interference-free.

XI. Minimal Additional Load for Resource-Poor Devices

The third requirement is to minimize the additional load for devices in the pervasive system which are not resourceful but execute pervasive applications. A practical realization should aim at requiring low additional effort such that the continuous execution of applications is not threatened.

XII. Availability of Application Coordination Functionality

The last requirement addresses the availability of application coordination. Pervasive systems can be highly dynamic and changes in the set of devices may happen unexpectedly. Consequently, the practical realization should enable a continuous provision of application coordination. For this purpose, it needs to be able to cope with unreliability of devices.

6.4. Component Placement

In this section, the practical realization of the framework for application coordination is discussed. The decisions are made to meet the requirements identified in the last section. They tailor the approach to the targeted systems. In the following, a brief overview of the entire process of application coordination is given. The data and task components which need to be deployed are depicted and the required data access and exchange are identified. Subsequently, the decisions for component placement and the points in time, when data is exchanged, are discussed for interference detection in Section 6.4.1 and interference resolution in Section 6.4.2.

Figure 6.1 gives an overview of the complete application coordination process. As discussed in Section 5.4.2, application coordination is split into two subprocesses, interference detection and interference resolution. The *interference detection* process is realized by the

6.4. Component Placement

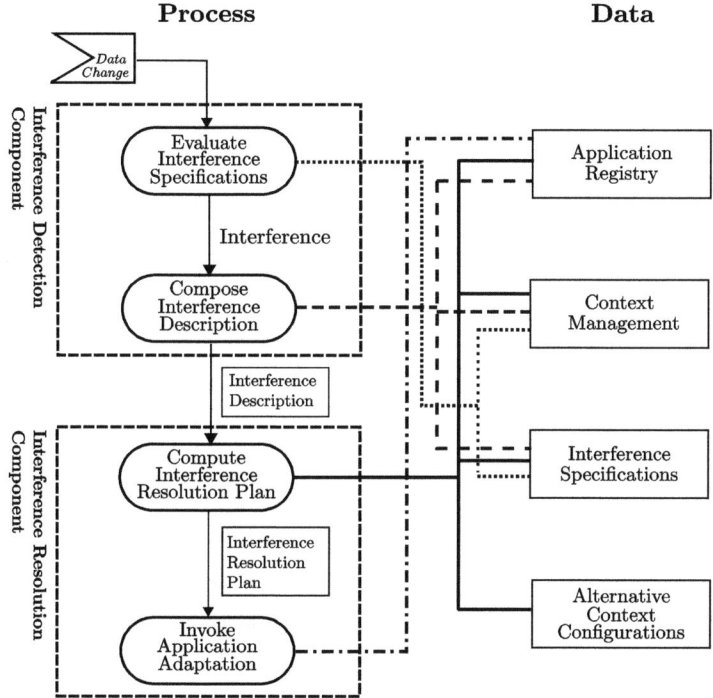

Figure 6.1.: Overview: Data Access

interference detection component. The process is invoked any time a change in the set of interference specifications or the context information happens. The interference detection component realizes two subprocesses: the evaluation of interference specifications and the composition of interference descriptions. For the evaluation of interference specifications, the process requires access to the set of interference specifications and information about the state of the context which is addressed by the interference specifications. If the evaluation yields a satisfied interference specification, an interference description must be composed. Since the description comprises the satisfied interference specification, the context information which has led to its satisfaction, and a list of all involved applications, this process requires access to the set of interference specifications, the context information, and the application registry. Once the interference description is composed the interference resolution process is invoked.

The *interference resolution* process is realized by the interference resolution component. It consists of two subprocesses. The first subprocess is the computation of the interference resolution plan. This subprocess requires access to all four data components, viz. the set of interference specifications, context information, the application registry, and the alternative configurations. As a result this subprocess yields an interference resolution plan which contains application assignments to solve a detected interference. The plan serves as an input for the second subprocess, the invocation of application adaptation. To retrieve the required contact information, the subprocess requires access to the application registry. Once the assignments have been sent to the applications, the process is finished.

In order to realize application coordination in practical pervasive systems, tasks and data must be deployed on devices. As discussed in Section 6.3, the approach must satisfy Requirements IX, X, XI, and XII. In the following, Sections 6.4.1 and 6.4.2 discuss the realization decisions for interference detection and interference resolution respectively.

6.4.1. Interference Detection

Figure 6.2 shows an overview of the component placement required for interference detection. For the practical realization, a centralized approach has been chosen. The interfer-

6.4. Component Placement

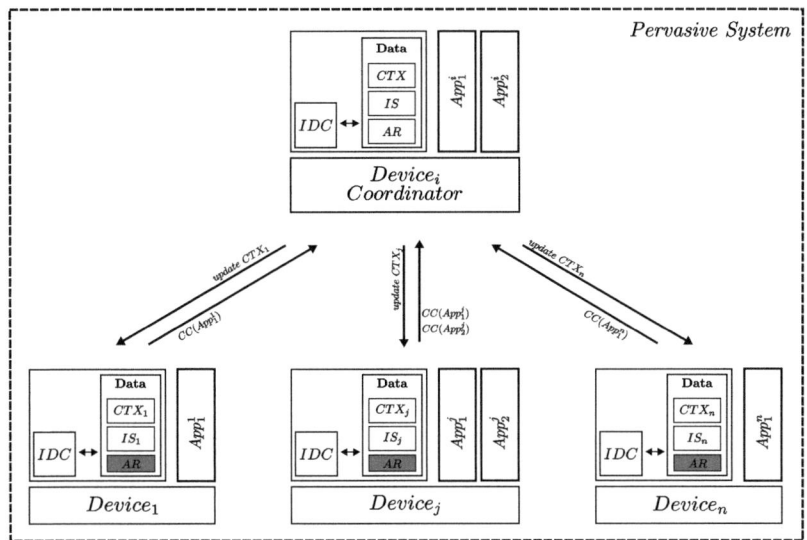

Figure 6.2.: Interference Detection: Component Placement

ence detection component IDC, which realizes the two subprocesses and all required data components – the set of interference specifications IS, the context information CTX, and the application registry AR – are placed on a resourceful device, the *coordinator* ($Device_i$). The coordinator is responsible for the detection of interferences that occur between applications executed on the devices $Device_1$, $Device_i$, $Device_j$, and $Device_n$.

The centralized placement of task and data components contributes to the satisfaction of Requirement IX. The requirement states that the time taken by the entire process should be minimized. The subsequent discussion exclusively focuses on optimizations which can be achieved through intelligent component placement and points in time when data is exchanged. Other optimizations such as the improvement of employed algorithms or data structures are not considered.

For interference detection, the process requires access to the set of interference specifications and the context information. If the data is not maintained centrally, interference detection requires network communication in order to collect the data distributed among multiple devices. Besides the interference specifications and context influences, this also involves the continuous collection of context information provided by sensors in the environment.

Focusing exclusively on component placement, the only possibility to optimize the time required for interference detection is the avoidance of network communication during the process. For this purpose, the interference detection component, the set of interference specifications, and the context information need to be placed centrally. The placement allows the execution of the interference process locally without the need to retrieve data over the network. All interference specifications which need to be evaluated are locally available as well as the context information for which the interference specifications are evaluated. Moreover, the centralized placement of task and data components allows interference detection to be triggered with a minimal delay, i.e. as soon as a change in the context information is observed.

A challenge of the centralized placement, however, is the currentness of data. Since interferences are detected based on the set of interference specifications and the data held in the context model, both data sets need to be up to date when the interference detection process is started. To keep data in the sets up to date, applications need to provide their interference specifications and context influences as soon as possible. This is realized by requiring applications to register at the coordinator as soon as they enter the pervasive system and to provide their active context configurations. The same holds for the case when an active context configuration changes. In order to process a detection as fast as possible, the application needs to send an update on its context configuration to the central entity immediately. Given that remote access is more time consuming than local operations, a centralized storage of the interference detection process, the context model including context influences, and a collection of all interference specifications on a single device satisfies Requirement IX. These decisions also suggest a centralized placement of the application registry on the coordinator. Consequently, the interference detection component can create an interference description with local data access.

6.4. Component Placement

In addition to the centralized placement of necessary components at the coordinator, each non-coordinator device is provided with the same functionality as the coordinator. The functionalities include the ability to set up a context model, the set of interference specifications, and the application registry as well as an instance of the interference detection component. The application registry AR is emphasized, as it is only used in case the device becomes coordinator. In addition to the functionalities, every non-coordinator holds a tailored copy of the context information maintained by the coordinator. The context information which is contained in the copy is determined by the interference specifications of applications executed on the device. As an example, the context information CTX_j on device j includes all context information that is addressed by the interference specifications of $App_1^j, \ldots, App_{i_j}^j$.

There are two reasons for the provision to non-coordinator devices of the functionalities and data required for interference detection. The first reason is to enable each device to locally detect interferences. Given the tailored copy of context information, each device can locally detect if it encounters an interference. The ability to detect encountered interferences enables applications to differentiate between actual interferences or natural context changes. While the former needs to be managed through application coordination, the latter is a situation for which a pervasive application has been designed. Consequently, the application can adapt itself to handle the natural context change without interaction with the coordinator.

The application can actively check for interferences it encounters and choose a context configuration and thus a functional configuration that does not lead to an interference. In the described setup, the application's ability to avoid interferences is limited. The application cannot determine if its execution will cause an interference with any other application in the pervasive system based on the reduced set of interference specifications.

The second reason for the provision of non-coordinator devices with respective functionalities is the realization of a backup mechanism. The backup mechanism enables the resumption of interference detection for the pervasive system if the current coordinator becomes unavailable. As discussed in detail in Section 6.5, a new coordinator is elected in the event that no coordinator exists. With the provision of coordinator functionality, every device is eligible to be elected as coordinator and thus to set up the required data structures and perform interference detection. However, in order to be a coordinator, a device needs to provide sufficient resources. If the resources of a device are so limited that it cannot act as a coordinator, it also does not need to be equipped with the respective functionality or data.

6.4.2. Interference Resolution

The interference resolution process consists of two subprocesses. At first, an interference resolution plan needs to be computed. The computation is performed according to one of the strategies which are set for the environment. To compute an interference resolution plan, the interference resolution component requires access to the context information, the set of interference specifications, the application registry, and the set of alternative application configurations. Once a resolution plan has been computed, the coordinator initiates the adaptation of applications according to the plan. For this purpose, it needs to retrieve contact information from the application registry.

The component deployment for interference detection results in a centralized placement of the set of interference specifications, the context information, and the application registry. Hence, a centralized placement of the task and data components required for interference resolution is reasonable. In addition to the three data components, the interference resolution component requires access to the alternative context configurations. Figure 6.3 shows the centralized placement for data. The interference resolution component IRC and all required data components – context information CTX, the set of interference specifications IS, the application registry AR, and the set of alternative application configurations ACC – have been placed on the *coordinator*.

The centralized placement and management of alternative application configurations contributes to the satisfaction of Requirement IX considering interference resolution. Due to the nature of the interference resolution plan computation, each alternative configuration may be analyzed several times. To avoid the retrieval of data via network commu-

6.4. Component Placement

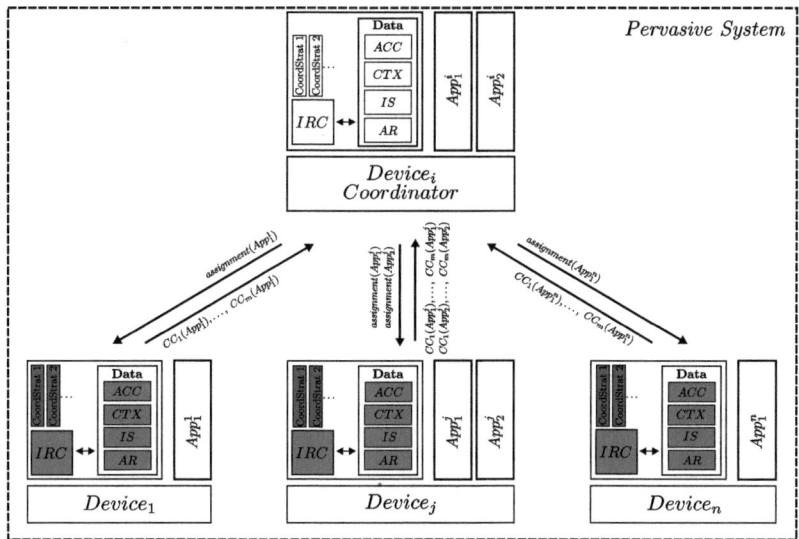

Figure 6.3.: Interference Resolution: Component Placement

nication on the critical path for every access, alternative context configurations should be locally available. Moreover, the point in time when applications compute and provide their alternative context configurations is a crucial factor considering the satisfaction of Requirement IX. The decision of whether to compute alternative context contributions or to provide them is a trade-off between Requirements XI and IX. To satisfy Requirement XI it is reasonable to request and compute alternative application configurations only when they are needed. The advantage of this proceeding is that the effort can be reduced. For example, it is possible to use a coordination strategy which allows the coordinator to pre-select those applications which are required to compute and provide their alternative context configurations. In the ideal case, alternative context configurations are computed and provided by a minimal set of applications. In the worst case, however, the requested alternative context configurations do not suffice to compute a resolution for an interference. The disadvantage of requesting further alternative context configurations contradicts Requirement IX. At first, the interference resolution plan computation is further delayed as context configurations need to be retrieved. Moreover, the process may be further delayed if the selected application needs to compute alternative context configurations first.

To avoid a delay, alternative context configurations should be provided by an application as soon as possible. A point in time when this proves reasonable is during an application's registration. An application registers as soon as it enters the environment. As a new environment often also implies a changed context, the application is likely to compute configurations for the changed execution environment. Consequently, the applications can determine alternative context configurations and provide them to the coordinator. This, however, implies that applications need to send updates in case their alternative context configurations change to keep updated information at the coordinator. The advantage of the proactive provision of alternative context configurations is that the interference resolution plan can be computed without the need to retrieve required information during the process. On the other hand, this may lead to unnecessary computations on the application side. If the adaptation of a certain application is never required, the computation of alternative context configurations only results in additional load. The determination of whether or not the computation of alternative context configurations is necessary is not possible before a solution to an interference is found. Thus, the trade-off lies between additional load for applications or a delayed interference resolution. However, requiring an application to compute alternative context configurations at a certain point in time may come at an inconvenient moment. Thus, it suggests to be more reasonable to have applications compute alternative context configurations when they enter the pervasive system and update them if necessary.

In order to provide a backup mechanism, all devices in the pervasive system are provided with the basic functionality to set up interference resolution. As shown in Figure 6.3, the elements are emphasized as they do not become active unless the device is selected as coordinator.

6.5. Dynamic Application Coordination

Figure 6.4 shows an overview of the component placement for the entire application coordination process, as presented in the preceding sections. All task and data components have been placed on a central element, the coordinator. The elements which are only used if the device becomes the coordinator are emphasized.

Due to the unreliability of devices in general pervasive systems, the coordinator cannot be guaranteed to remain within the system throughout the entire system life cycle. Consequently, measures need to be taken to cope with dynamic environments in order to satisfy Requirement XII. In the time span, when no coordinator is available, application coordination cannot be performed. Moreover, if the coordinator leaves the environment unexpectedly, an non-completed application coordination process may be aborted. In order to satisfy Requirement X, application coordination is resumed by setting up a new coordinator. For this purpose, every device in the pervasive system is provided with the ability to set up application-coordination-specific data models and to perform the tasks of interference detection and resolution.

In order to set up a new coordinator, several steps are required. Figure 6.5 shows the process for the setup of a new coordinator. The process is subdivided into four phases, the *Election Phase*, the *Initiation Phase*, the *Registration Phase*, and the *Coordination Phase*. The setup process is triggered as soon as the current coordinator leaves the pervasive system. If the coordinator leaves the environment in a planned way, it can initiate a new coordinator selection. If the coordinator leaves the environment unexpectedly, the election is initiated as soon as a device observes that no coordinator is present.

In the *Election Phase* a new coordinator must be selected which fulfills the task of application coordination. Moreover, all devices must be aware of the new coordinator. For this purpose, a number of algorithmic approaches exist which realize the election of a coordinator. In this process, devices are compared with respect to their suitability of performing the role as a coordinator. The suitability of a device may depend on different aspects. A very prominent example is the *lowest id* approach of Ephremides *et al.* [EWB87] which is used to select nodes with specific responsibilities in MANETs. The

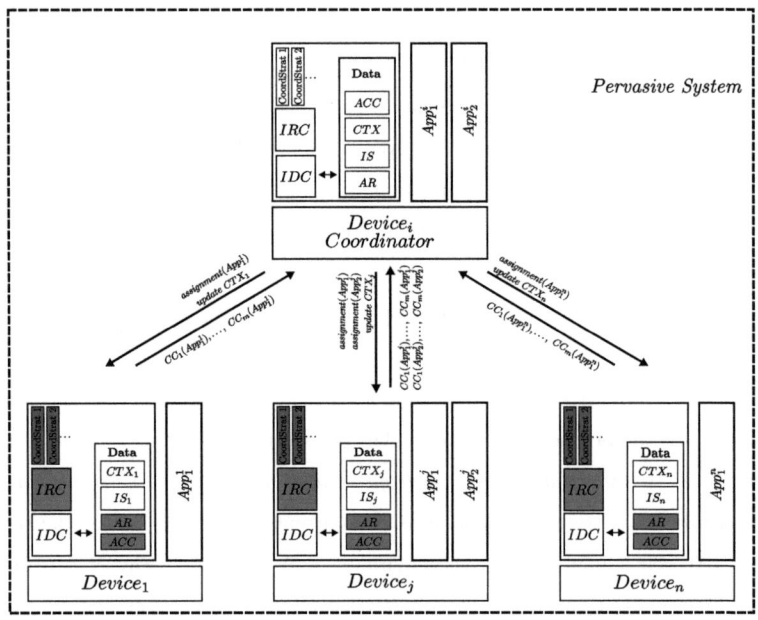

Figure 6.4.: Application Coordination: Component Placement

6.5. Dynamic Application Coordination

approach is based on the assumption that every node in the network has a unique id. If a new responsible node is required, the device with the lowest id is selected as responsible device. Another example is the one presented by Schiele [Sch07] which uses the remaining energy of a node as decision factor. An alternative metric is that presented by Basu *et al.* [BKL01] which uses the mobility of nodes as a decision factor for the selection of a dedicated node in ad hoc networks.

For application coordination the suitability of a device with respect to performing the coordinator role is primarily determined through its resourcefulness. The coordinator device needs to have enough resources in order to fulfill the tasks of interference detection and resolution. Furthermore, it may be reasonable to select a reliable device in order to overcome the need for repeated coordinator election. Since the existence of a reliable device cannot be assumed the decision was made to use the election algorithm based on the lowest id. This approach provides good results in smart environments as well as in smart peer groups. In smart environments the devices with the lowest id are those that are part of the installed infrastructure and thus are reliable. In smart peer groups the resourceful device with the lowest id is likely to be the device of the user who initiated the creation of the smart peer group.

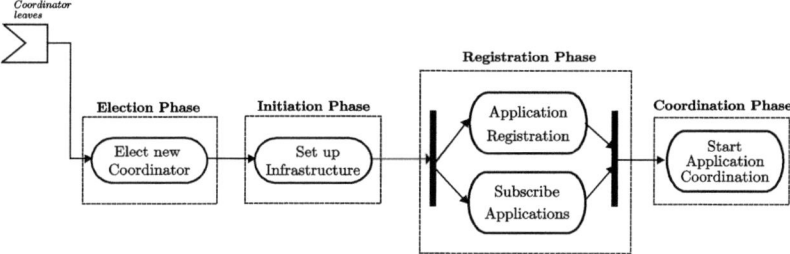

Figure 6.5.: Coordinator Setup Process

Once the coordinator has been selected, the *Initiation Phase* is entered. In this phase the new coordinator is set up. This includes the instantiation of all task and data components which are required by the coordinator. With respect to task components, the coordinator needs to initiate the interference detection and resolution component. Furthermore, the data components, context information, interference specifications, alternative application configurations, and application registry need to be instantiated. The outcome of this phase is a coordinator which is ready to start coordinating applications in the pervasive system.

The *Registration Phase* is the third phase in the overall process of the coordinator setup. This phase is similar to the initial coordinator setup. In this phase all applications are required to register at the new coordinator. The registration process serves the purpose of providing the new coordinator with the data required for application coordination. Moreover, sensors need to be registered if a device possesses sensors. Since the coordinator has changed, sensors also need to change the address point to which they provide data. Secondly, applications register their context configurations. In the process of adding interference specifications, the new coordinator also subscribes devices to context information required for the evaluation of the local interference specifications.

With the initialization of the data components with required data, the setup of the new coordinator is complete. Consequently, application coordination can be resumed and the *Coordination Phase* is entered. The new coordinator is now responsible for the detection and resolution of interferences in the pervasive system. The responsibility ends in case the coordinator becomes unavailable.

To summarize this chapter, the realization of the application coordination framework for practical pervasive systems was discussed. At first, the reliability and resourcefulness of devices were identified as system characteristics which have an influence on the practical realization. Next, general pervasive systems were analyzed with respect to the characteristics and requirements towards a practical realization were identified. Finally, the component placement for application coordination was presented and an approach for dynamic environments was introduced. Through the realization decisions, Requirements IX through XII could be satisfied.

7. Protoype

This chapter presents COMITY, the prototypical implementation of the concepts introduced in Chapters 5 and 6. Section 7.1 gives an overview of the coordinator and its components, Configuration and Application Management, Context Management, Interference Detection, and Interference Resolution. Subsequently, Section 7.2 describes the implementation of context configurations, before the four parts are presented in Section 7.3 through 7.6. The chapter closes with a description of the implementation of the coordinator in BASE, a system software for pervasive computing, realizing application coordination in a practical pervasive system.

7.1. Coordinator Overview

Figure 7.1 shows an UML [Gro07] class diagram of the COMITY prototype which has been implemented in Java. The central class of the prototype is the *Coordinator* which implements the interface *ICoordinator*. The interface offers all methods to applications which are required for application coordination and which can be called on the coordinator:

register(cbInfo, ContextConfiguration):appID The register method registers an application at the coordinator for application coordination. It is the first method, a pervasive application must call on the coordinator. The method requires two parameters. First, an application provides its callback information. The callback information enables the coordinator to contact the application in case of an interference. The second parameter is the application's active context configuration. With a successful registration, the coordinator ensures that the application interferences

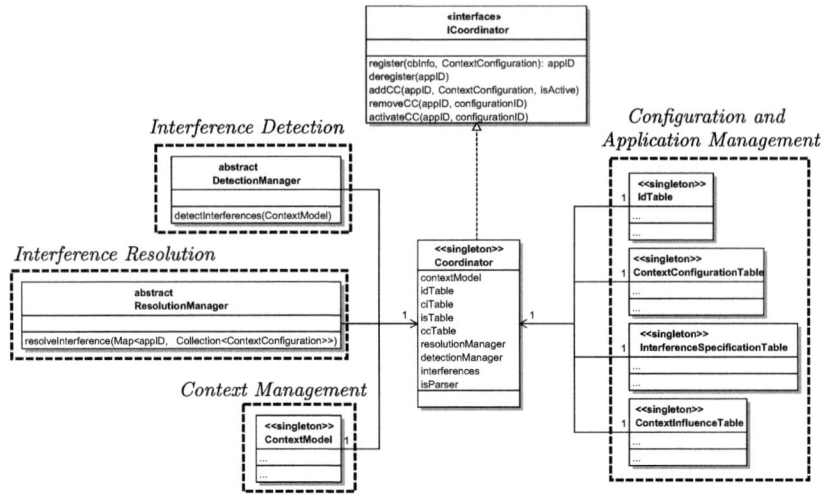

Figure 7.1.: UML: Coordinator Overview

are detected and measures are taken to resolve them. A successful registration returns an `appID`. The `appID` identifies the application at the coordinator and needs to be used for all methods called on the coordinator subsequent to the application's registration. In case the registration fails, an exception is thrown.

deregister(appID) The counterpart to the `register` method is the `deregister` method. The method takes a single parameter, namely the `appID`. A call of the `deregister` method on the coordinator removes an application from application coordination. It results in the deletion of all information associated with the application.

addCC(appID, ContextConfiguration, isActive) The third method which is provided by the coordinator allows applications to add further context configurations to the coordinator. As parameters, the method requires the `appID`, the context configuration and a flag which states if the context configuration is to be added as an active one. In case the flag is set to false, the context configuration is added as an alternative context configuration. The number of alternative context configurations

7.1. Coordinator Overview

an application can add to the coordinator is not restricted. In case the flag is set to true, the currently active context configuration is deactivated and the new context configuration is activated since only one configuration can be active per application at any given time. The method throws an exception if the configuration could not be successfully added.

removeCC(appID, configurationID) As applications can add context configurations to the coordinator, they can likewise remove them. As parameters this method requires the appID and the configurationID. The configuration identifier needs to be provided by an application itself in order to distinguish between the configurations added to the coordinator. In case an applications tries to delete an active context configuration, the operation fails and an exception is thrown. This is due to the fact that each application needs to have one configuration active in order to participate in application coordination. If the application removes an alternative configuration, the configuration is simply deleted.

activateCC(appID, configurationID) The last method which can be called on the coordinator by pervasive applications is the activation of a configuration which has already been added to the coordinator. The activate method requires the appID and the configurationID as parameters. In the activation process, the coordinator deactivates the currently active configuration and activates the configuration with configurationID. In case no configuration can be found with the respective identifier, the method fails and an exception is thrown.

The interface provides all methods that allow applications to register themselves and to manage their active and alternative context configurations. The collection of context configurations constitute the coordinator's data basis to perform all tasks of application coordination. To manage context configuration information and to realize application coordination, the coordinator comprises four parts which are illustrated in Figure 7.1. The management of context configuration information is realized by a collection of classes combined into *Configuration and Application Management* and is described in detail in Section 7.3. The second part is *Context Management* and is addressed in Section 7.4. While the focus of application and configuration and context management is the maintenance of data, *Interference Detection* and *Interference Resolution* realize their corresponding tasks. Interference detection and interference resolution are discussed in Section 7.5 and Section 7.6 respectively. In the following, the realization of context configurations is presented first to provide a basic understanding of the data type in the following discussion.

7.2. Context Configuration

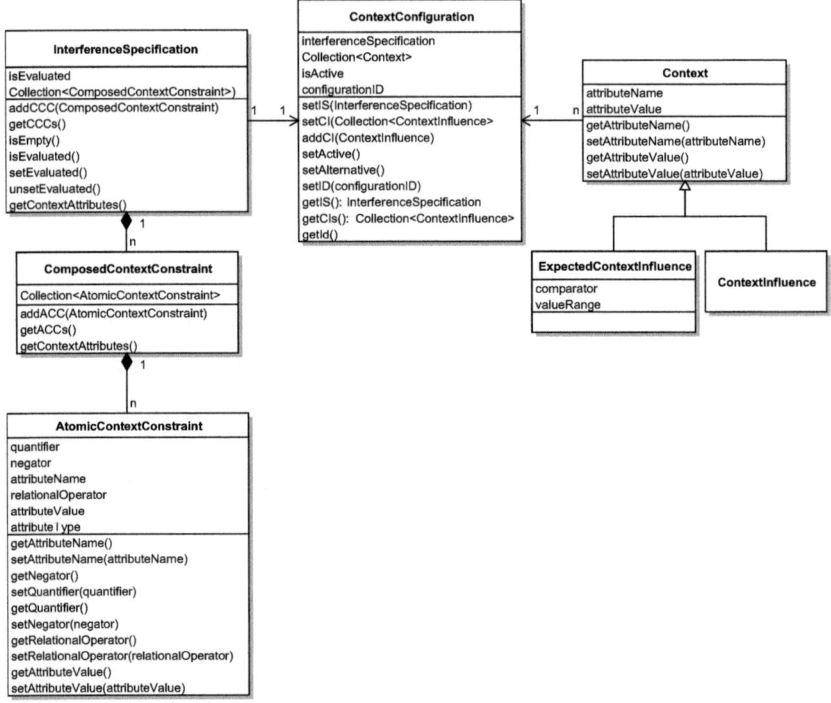

Figure 7.2.: UML: Context Configuration

Context configurations provide the information based on which application coordination is realized. Figure 7.2 shows a UML diagram for the classes which compose a context

7.3. Configuration and Application Management

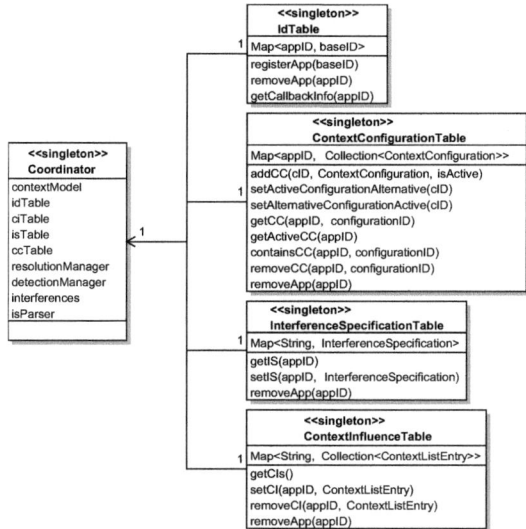

Figure 7.3.: UML: Coordinator Management Tables

configuration. A context configuration consists of an *InterferenceSpecification* and a collection of objects of type *Context*.

The *InterferenceSpecification* is realized in accordance with Definition 4. It is a collection of *ComposedContextConstraint*s which in turn are collections of *AtomicContextConstraint*s. An *AtomicContextConstraint* comprises a quantifier, a negator, its attribute name, a relational operator, the attribute value, and its attribute type. The specific attribute name, the viable relational operators, and the attribute type depend on the context ontology which is used by the coordinator.

Context objects can be specialized into *ExpectedContextInfluence*s or *ContextInfluence*s as specified in Definitions 5 and 6. The former allows the definition of range values to represent anticipated context influences. The latter explicitly specifies the actual context influences of the application.

7.3. Configuration and Application Management

In order to manage the information provided in context configurations, the coordinator maintains a set of management tables, namely the *IdTable*, the *ContextConfigurationTable*, the *InterferenceSpecificationTable*, and the *ContextInfluenceTable*, as shown in Figure 7.3. The tables allow easy access to information required for regular operations such as adding and removing context configurations, or retrieving an application's active one.

The *IdTable* serves the purpose of keeping track of registered applications. It holds all application ids assigned by the coordinator including the application's callback information. To manage the table, methods to register and remove applications and to get their callback information are provided.

The *ContextConfigurationTable* stores all context configurations of registered applications. This includes one active context configuration per application and an arbitrary number of alternative context configurations. In order to realize the functionality of the methods offered by the coordinator interface, the *ContextConfigurationTable* offers respective methods to add, remove, and change the status of active and alternative configurations.

For efficiency reasons of interference detection and resolution, information of active context configurations is stored in additional tables, the *InterferenceSpecificationTable* and the *ContextInfluenceTable*. The *InterferenceSpecificationTable* holds all interference specifications which are currently active for the pervasive system. This provides fast access to the set of interference specifications which need to be evaluated in the interference detection process. The *ContextInfluenceTable* enables the tracking of active context influences which have been added as context to the context model. It allows the coordinator to quickly access an application's context influences in the context model without additional search effort and to remove them if required. In order to manage both tables, methods to set and remove interference specifications and context influences are provided.

7.4. Context Management

The context influences of an application's active context configuration are handled by the configuration and application management as well as by the context management. This is due to the fact that context influences as part of a context configuration are also part of the context. Thus, context influences are managed in the respective tables but are also added to the context model as context information.

The current state of the environment in which pervasive applications are executed is held in the context model. However, context influences are not the only elements which are added to the context model. To maintain the current context state, a variety of sensors may report their information to the context model. The number of sensors is not restricted and different sensors as well as applications can report values for identical context attributes. Thus, in order to obtain a consistent context state, the context model needs to merge these values and decide on the actual state of an attribute. The prototype has also been designed such that pervasive applications can use the context model as a primary source for context information for their context-awareness.

The context model is built according to an ontology. For this purpose, Section 7.4.1 first introduces the ontology which has been developed as part of the prototype, before the context model is discussed in Section 7.4.2.

7.4.1. Context Ontology

A challenge for application coordination is the common addressing of the shared context. In order to detect and resolve interferences, the data held in the context model and the data provided in the context configurations need to be compliant. For this purpose, a context ontology was developed. The ontology provides a common vocabulary for the context which is shared by applications in the pervasive system. To achieve a common addressing, the context model as well as the elements used in context configurations, must comply with the context ontology.

The ontology was developed on the basis of the ontology presented by J. Frankenbach [Fra10]. The ontology is tailored for application coordination and is composed of parts of the ontologies SOUPA [CPFJ04], CONON [WZGP04] and the ontology developed by Korpipää [KMK+03]. Furthermore, the ontology was extended based on sensor class research in pervasive systems conducted by Beigl et al. [BKZD04]. The sensor classes, which are important for interference management, are *audio*, *light*, *temperature*, and *humidity*. All of these classes have been added to the ontology and have been refined where needed.

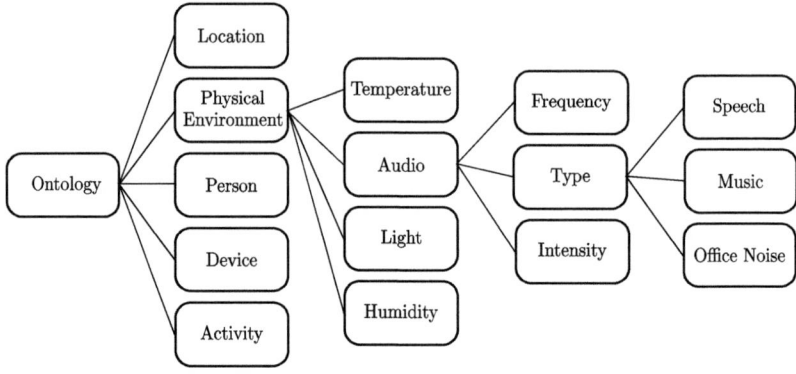

Figure 7.4.: Context Ontology Extract

A graphical overview of an extraction of the ontology is illustrated in Figure 7.4. The figure shows a selection of entities which are important for application coordination. The ontology extraction shows that the context of an application is mainly determined by five classes namely *Location, Physical Environment, Person, Device,* and *Activity*.

The *Location* of an application is a major characteristic as it determines its physical location and thus the context it shares. Recall that the use of a location model was assumed in the system model in order to provide physical spaces with a symbolic reference. Hence, the prototype uses a room-centric approach to model physical spaces. As a consequence, the attributes of the room compose the context of a pervasive application. The attributes are the room's *Physical Environment*, the *Person*s residing in the room, the *Device*s within the room, and the *Activity* indicated for the room. The *Physical Environment* can further be subdivided into *Temperature, Audio, Light* and *Humidity*. Each attribute can have further characteristics. As an example, *Audio* is further subdivided into *Frequency*,

7.4. Context Management

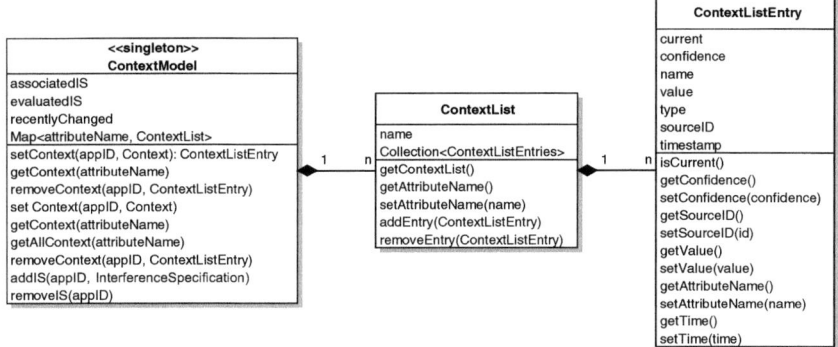

Figure 7.5.: UML: Context Model

Type, and *Intensity* where *Speech*, *Music*, and *Office Noises* are added as possible audio types. Moreover, the ontology only comprises context entities which have been identified to be subject to interferences. Since the development of a comprehensive and complete ontology was not the focus of this thesis, the ontology remains on a prototypical level required to implement application coordination.

7.4.2. Context Model

The context ontology serves as an input for the constructor for a *ContextModel* object. The constructor parses the ontology, creates the respective context attributes and generates consistency check rules based for viable value ranges and value types. This allows it to automatically check if a context model entry complies with the ontology. As an example, the context ontology defines a context "physical environment" with an attribute "audio" which has a "type" which can take the values "speech", "music", and "office noise". When the context model is set up, the constructor creates the context attribute "physical_environment.audio.type". Furthermore, a consistency check is added for the *setContext* method that checks if the value takes one of the pre-defined possibilities.

The collection of all context attributes composes the context. When a context attribute value is set, the context model stores a timestamp, the source of the context, and the confidence of the source. A source can be any kind of sensor, a context inference engine, or an application in the pervasive system. The confidence of the source determines the probability that the reported value is correct and is required for the computation of a consistent context state.

Since several sources can report context information, the context model can hold several entries per context attribute. This relationship is also reflected in the UML diagram in Figure 7.5. The *ContextModel* is an aggregation of *ContextList* objects. A *ContextList* object represents one specific context attribute and holds all entries related to that attribute realized through *ContextListEntry* objects.

The resulting internal structure of the context model is illustrated in Table 7.1. The table shows that each context attribute can have several entries, the *ContextListEntries* which compose the *ContextList* of the attribute. The first entry in each list holds the actual value of the attribute and is indicated by the final flag. The actual value is computed by the context model on the basis of the context information provided by the various sources. This context information is stored in the subsequent rows where *final* is set to false. Every entry consists of the *timestamp* when the context information was added to the context model, the *source id* of the context source, the *confidence* that the value is correct, the *value*, and the value *type*. The final-flagged entry does not hold a source id. However, the sources which have contributed to the context state can be retrieved from the list.

The design of the context model to have several entries per context attribute realizes two objectives: 1) The context model needs to be able to determine and communicate the actual state of the context. For example, if an application requires knowledge about the current temperature, the context model needs to be able to service this query. 2) For interference resolution, the coordinator needs to be able to retrieve all parties that contribute to a certain context state. In the example given above, the context model returns that the value of attribute "audio.volume" is 55 *dB*. For interference resolution, however, the coordinator needs to know all parties that contribute to the context state. The table shows that two applications have an influence on the audio volume. The source

7.5. Interference Detection

attribute	\multicolumn{7}{c}{Context Model}

attribute	final	timestamp	source id	confidence	value	type
temperature	true	16:13:15:045	-	1.0	19.0	celsius
	false	16:13:14:812	app5	1.0	19.0	celsius
	false	16:13:14:035	sen7	0.9	19.0	celsius
	false	16:13:14:099	sen3	0.88	19.2	celsius
audio.volume	true	16:13:14:015	-	1.0	55	dB
	false	16:13:14:001	app2	1.0	55	dB
	false	16:13:15:015	app3	1.0	45	dB
	false	16:13:15:014	sen1	0.8	54	dB
light.intensity	true	16:13:10:077	-	0.9	100	lx
	false	16:13:14:990	sen4	0.9	100	lx
	false	16:13:13:045	sen5	0.9	90	lx

Table 7.1.: Internal Structure of the Context Model

app2 influences the context with 55 *dB* while source *app3* influences the context with 45 *dB*. In addition, the noise level is captured by the sensor *sen1* and is reported to the context model.

In case an interference occurs due to the value of "audio.volume" being greater than 30*dB*, it will not suffice to exclusively adapt *app2* for a resolution. The coordinator needs to know that two applications contribute to the current state of the audio.volume attribute in order to compute an interference resolution plan. The sensor, in contrast, only reports the context and cannot be included for resolution purposes.

7.5. Interference Detection

The third building block of the prototype is the *Interference Detection*. As shown in Figure 7.6, the abstract class *DetectionManager* contains a single method, namely *detectInterferences* which requires the context model as input. The current version of the prototype implements two variants of interference detection, the *BasicInterferenceDetection* and the *OptimizedInterferenceDetection*.

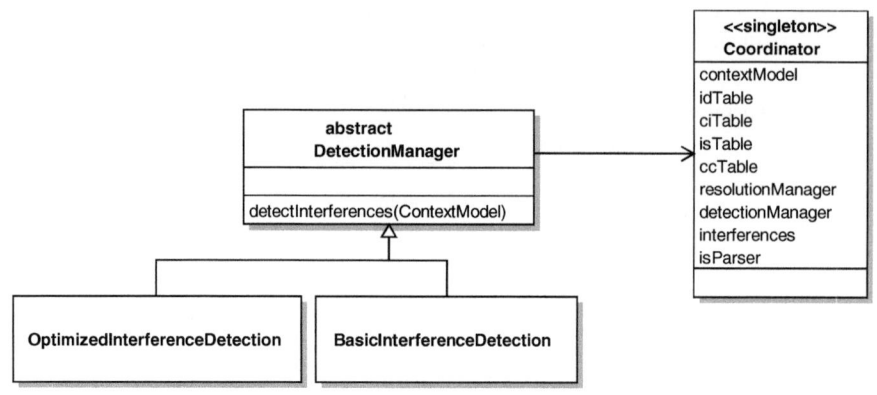

Figure 7.6.: UML: Interference Detection

Algorithm 5: *detectInterferences*

Input: IS, CTX

Output: $Collection<InterferenceDescription>$

1 **begin**
2   **if** $OPTIMIZED$ **then**
3        $IS \leftarrow filterRelevantIS(IS)$
4     $result \leftarrow$ **new** $Collection()$
5   **for** $IS_{App_i} \in IS$ **do**
6        $iDes_{App_i} \leftarrow \textbf{hasInterference}(IS_{App_i}, CTX)$
7     $add(result, iDes_{App_i})$
8   **return** $result$

Both algorithms are summarized in Algorithm 5. As input the algorithms take the set of active interference specifications IS and the current context CTX which is held in the context model. The *BasicInterferenceDetection* checks every interference specification in the set of active interference specifications for satisfaction by the current context. For this purpose, the algorithm calls the *hasInterference* method which evaluates one interference specification for the current context and returns an interference description. The interference description states the context which leads to the satisfaction of the

7.5. Interference Detection

interference specification as well as the sources of the context. In case the interference specification is not satisfied, the interference description is empty.

The *hasInterference* method is described in Algorithm 6. To compose the interference description, the *hasInterference* method breaks down the interference specification in *AtomicContextConstraint* objects and checks if these are satisfied by the current context. Consider the example where an *AtomicContextConstraint* has the form `audio.volume > 30 dB`. The method then retrieves the actual value of `audio.volume` from the context model and checks if it meets the constraint. If the actual value is greater than $30dB$, an interference description is composed. The source of the context is identified and the context as well as its possibly several sources are added to the interference description. Thus, the result of the *detectInterferences* algorithm is a collection of interference descriptions. In the collection, each description represent one satisfied interference specification. The collection serves as input for interference resolution.

Algorithm 6: *hasInterference*

Input: IS, CTX

Output: $Collection<InterferenceDescription>$

1 **begin**
2     $iDes \leftarrow$ **new** $InterferenceDescription()$
3     $CCCs \leftarrow getComposedContextConstraints(IS)$
4   **for** $CCC \in CCCs$ **do**
5        $ACCs \leftarrow getAtomicContextConstraints(CCC)$
6   **for** $ACC \in ACCs$ **do**
7            $CTX_{ACC} \leftarrow getContext(getAttributeName(ACC))$
8   **if** $satisfies(CTX, ACC)$ **then**
9                $add(iDes, (CTX, getSource(CTX)))$
10   **return** $iDes$

In addition to the basic interference detection, the prototype also implements an optimized version. The optimized version reduces the number of interference specifications which must be evaluated in the interference detection process. The reduction is based on

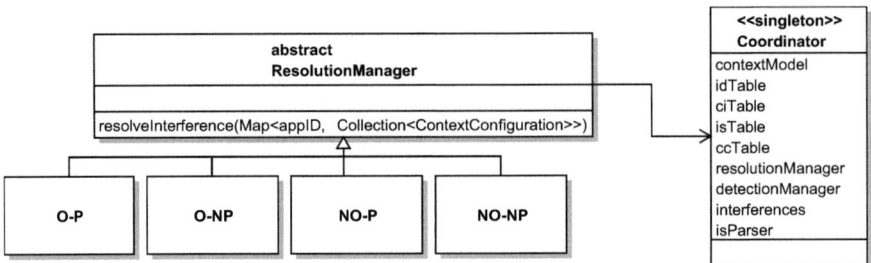

Figure 7.7.: UML: Interference Resolution

the following idea: The evaluation of an interference specification will always yield the same result unless the values of the context attributes it constrains are changed. Therefore, it is reasonable to evaluate only those interference specifications which may have been affected by a context change.

To realize this, two additional mechanisms were implemented. At first, when an interference specification is registered at the coordinator, the coordinator retrieves the addressed attributes and creates links between these attributes and the interference specification. This enables the coordinator to have a direct access to all interference specifications which include a particular context attribute. Secondly, the context model was provided with the ability to track which context attributes have been changed recently. A context attribute has been changed recently, if it was altered after interference detection was performed the last time. If *detectInterferences* is called, the coordinator iterates over the set of recently changed attributes, retrieves the associated interference specifications and clears the set. Subsequently, the retrieved interference specifications are evaluated for the current context.

7.6. Interference Resolution

The last building block of the prototype is *Interference Resolution*. The UML overview of *Interference Resolution* is shown in Figure 7.7. The abstract class *ResolutionManager* has a single method namely *resolveInterference* which takes a map of application ids and

7.6. Interference Resolution

their context configurations as input. The prototype implements four different algorithms to compute an interference resolution plan, viz. NO-NP, O-NP, NO-P, and O-P where O stands for the ordering heuristic, P stands for pruning, and N is the negator. NO-NP realizes a chronological backtracking, O-NP an informed backtracking using the ordering heuristic, NO-P an informed backtracking that uses pruning, and O-P an informed backtracking that uses both ordering and pruning.

Algorithm 7: *resolveInterference*

Input: *matrix : ContextConfigurationMatrix*
Output: *com : ContextConfigurationCombination*

1 **begin**
2   **if** *ORDERING* **then**
3 | *matrix* ← *sortAppsByInvolvementASC(matrix)*
4   *com* ← *initialCombination(matrix)*
5   **while** *hasNextCombination(com)* **do**
6   **if** *PRUNING* **then**
7 | *com* ← *nextPrunedCombination(matrix, com)*
8   **else**
9 | *com* ← *nextCombination(matrix, com)*
10   **if** *isInterferenceFree(com)* **then**
11 | **return** *com*
12   **return** ∅

The four variations are summarized in Algorithm 7. A variation can be obtained by setting ORDERING and PRUNING as required. Recall that the algorithm takes a matrix of context configurations as input. In case ORDERING and PRUNING are disabled, the algorithm realizes a chronological backtracking. The algorithm terminates if either an interference-free combination is found or all combinations have been checked and no solution could be found. The four resolution algorithms were introduced and discussed in detail as part of the theoretical framework in Section 5.4.2.5. For this purpose, the algorithms are not described in this section. For detailed information refer to Section 5.4.2.5.

7.7. Coordinator as a Service

In order to realize application coordination in practical pervasive systems, the coordinator has been implemented using a middleware. For the prototype the middleware BASE [BSGR03] has been selected as it has been specifically designed to meet the requirements of pervasive computing. It has a lightweight but extensible core based on a micro-broker approach. This allows BASE to be operated on resource-poor devices, such as embedded sensors, but it also supports the addition of costly functionalities to be run on full-fledged devices such as desktop computers.

Devices which are in communication range with each other and which are equipped with the BASE software are able to form a spontaneous network. BASE supports basic functionalities to manage the network, e.g. a device discovery and registry. It is able to dynamically detect new devices and to integrate them into the network making them available to all connected BASE instances. Likewise, BASE keeps the device registry up to date and removes devices which no longer exist. Once a network has been established, BASE instances are able to communicate with each other on a peer-to-peer basis.

In order to build and execute pervasive applications, BASE uses a service abstraction to model functionalities and capabilities in a common way and to provide a uniform access. Thus, remote services can be accessed via local proxies. The actual call on a remote service is realized by the BASE middleware. BASE has been designed to shield applications from the management of communication. Using BASE, an application can communicate with remote instances not having to manage communication technology, the interoperability protocols, or the communication models. As a consequence, pervasive applications are not aware of how their communication with remote devices is realized.

Figure 7.8 shows the coordinator as a BASE service. The coordinator is indicated through an emphasized border. In order to implement the coordinator as a service, a stub and a skeleton need to be generated and its interface needs to be exported in the BASE Service Registry. As a BASE service, the coordinator and the methods defined by its interface are available to all other BASE instances.

In order to be used by applications, the BASE application model was extended through

7.7. Coordinator as a Service

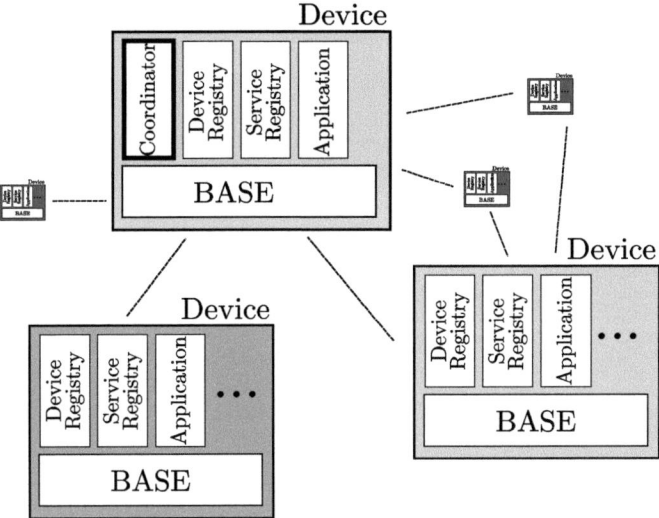

Figure 7.8.: Coordinator as BASE Service

a routine that automatically detects the coordinator, registers the application and provides its context configurations. In case no coordinator is found, the application initiates a coordinator election as described in Section 6.5.

To summarize the chapter, a prototypical implementation of the application coordination framework and its concepts has been presented. Besides the realization of the conceptual components described in Section 5.2, the coordinator is provided with additional tables. These tables enable easy access to information of active context configurations to support the execution of frequent operations. For context management, a context ontology was introduced and the internal structure of the context model was discussed. Furthermore, the implementation of the algorithms for interference detection and resolution were presented. The outcome of this chapter is a functioning prototype that is able to coordinate applications in pervasive systems. In order to integrate the functionality of application coordination in a real pervasive system, the coordinator was implemented as a BASE service.

8. Evaluation

This chapter evaluates the prototype which was presented in Chapter 7. The goal of this chapter is to assess the concepts which were developed in this thesis and to show the utilizability of the coordinator for practical pervasive systems. For this purpose, Section 8.1 first discusses the memory requirements of the coordinator in detail in dependence on the number of active applications and their context configurations. Subsequently, Section 8.2 evaluates the prototype with respect to its performance. At first, the critical path of application coordination is analyzed. Afterwards, measurements for the implemented interference detection and interference resolution algorithms are conducted and the results are discussed.

8.1. Memory Requirements and Overhead

The first evaluation addresses the memory requirements of the coordinator and the overhead it causes. Firstly, the memory requirements of the classes that compose the coordinator are determined in dependence of active and alternative context configurations. Secondly, conceivable examples of context configurations and the resulting load for the coordinator are discussed. Moreover, the resulting load is set in relation to the memory requirements of the middleware BASE to determine the overhead. Finally, the message overhead that is caused through the use of the coordinator in a pervasive system realized with BASE is analyzed.

In order to determine the memory requirements, a footprint of the prototype has been measured using the Java profiler Java VisualVM which is part of JDK. The classes that compose the prototype and their memory requirements are shown in Table 8.1. The table

Class	Size in Bytes
Coordinator	120
IdTable	$16 + (Size(CallBackInfo) + Size(Length(ID))) \cdot \#Apps$
CCTable	$16 + Size(CC_{any}) \cdot \#CC_{any}/App \cdot \#Apps$
ContextModel	$8 + Size(ContextList) \cdot \#CTXAttribute$
ISTable	$16 + Size(IS_{active}) \cdot \#Apps$
CITable	$16 + Size(ContextListEntry) \cdot \#Apps$

Table 8.1.: Memory Requirements: Coordinator Classes

states the size of each class in bytes in dependence on active and alternative context configurations.

As described in Chapter 7, the coordinator maintains different tables to manage application and context configuration information. The *IdTable* enables the coordinator to store coordination-specific ids and the callback information. As a consequence, the memory requirements are computed accordingly in addition to a base value of 16 bytes. The *CCTable* stores all context configurations of applications, the active as well as the alternative ones. Thus, the memory requirements are determined as a product of the size of context configurations, the number of context configurations per application and the number of active applications in the system. The size of the context model is determined through the number of context attributes maintained by the context model and the number of entries per attribute. Recall that for interference resolution, every context list holds one entry per source that reports a value for the respective attribute. The *ISTable* and *CITable* provide the coordinator with easy and efficient access to currently active configurations. This includes access to active interference specifications in the *ISTable* and the access to active context influences which are stored as context in the context model and referenced in the *CITable*. Hence, the memory requirements of the *ISTable* are determined through a base of 16 bytes plus the product of active interference specifications and the number of active applications in the pervasive system. The size of *CITable* is composed of a base of 16 bytes plus the product of the size of a *ContextListEntry* and the number of active applications.

8.1. Memory Requirements and Overhead

Class	Size in Bytes
ContextConfiguration (CC)	24+ *Size(IS)* + *Size(CI)*
InterferenceSpecification (IS)	$16 + \#CCC \cdot (16 + \#ACC \cdot 24)$
ContextInfluences (CI)	16
ContextList	$16 + 32 \cdot \# \ CTXEntries$
ContextListEntry	32

Table 8.2.: Memory Requirements: ContextConfiguration and ContextList

The formulas to compute the size of context configurations, context lists, and context list entries are given in Table 8.2. For example, a single *ContextListEntry* has a size of 32 bytes. Hence, the memory requirements of a *ContextList* is determined through the number and size of *ContextListEntry* objects plus a base of 16 bytes.

In order to give an idea for the real size of the coordinator which manages a number of applications and their context configurations, an example is described in the following: assuming the interference specification of the context configuration consists of 4 composed context constraints with 4 atomic context constraints each and assuming furthermore that the context configuration comprises 4 context influences. Thus, the overall size of the context configuration is 552 bytes. The resulting sizes for the coordinator classes are shown in Table 8.3. For the computations, the coordinator was assumed to manage a number of 0, 10, 25, 50, and 100 applications where each application had 1 active and 3 alternative context configurations.

Load	BASE	COMITY	Overhead
0	290kB	160B	0.0005 %
10	290kB	33428B	11.26 %
25	290kB	82418B	27.75 %
50	290kB	164068B	55.25 %
100	290kB	327368B	110.24 %

Table 8.3.: Memory Requirements and Overhead

The numbers in the table indicate that the memory requirements of COMITY grow with an increasing number of registered context configurations. Furthermore, the table shows the memory requirements for the middleware BASE and the overhead that is caused when the coordinator is used. The middleware has been chosen as comparison to give an idea for the size of a system software. Depending on the functionalities, the size of the system software may vary significantly. The selected configuration of BASE, however, provides a minimal configuration in order to manage pervasive systems and to enable communication in dynamic environments. The minimal configuration does not support the automatic configuration of applications or their adaptation. However, additional functionality will only add to the memory requirements of BASE.

According to the table, a minimal BASE configuration has a memory requirement of approximately 290kB. Running as a BASE service, a pure COMITY without data adds up to 160 bytes. In the initial setup, COMITY causes a minimal overhead. However, without any data the coordinator is not able to coordinate applications and with every context configuration that is added to the coordinator its memory requirement grows. In the described example, an overhead of about 11% is produced for a set of 10 applications. Recall that every application has 1 active and 3 alternative context configurations. To manage 50 applications in this scenario, the coordinator produces an overhead of about 55% in comparison to BASE. Thus, the memory requirements of BASE/COMITY add up to around 450kB when managing 50 applications. In today's pervasive systems, however, such a size is manageable by typical devices. Given that current smartphones such as the Samsung Galaxy S III [SEC] or the HTC One X+ [Cor] have a RAM of 1GB size, devices in a pervasive systems have sufficient resources (cf. Section 6.1) to host a coordinator.

Besides the memory requirements, the additional message load which is produced by the coordinator was investigated and compared to the pure BASE. In order to manage and keep the network up to date, BASE sends messages to and receives messages from all BASE instances in the system. The detection cycle is performed every 100ms. The time has been set in order to balance the tradeoff between network traffic and the refresh period for services within the network. For n BASE instances this results in $2(n-1)$ messages per instance adding up to $O(n^2)$ messages. The realization of the coordinator as a BASE service does not result in any extra messages. Since each BASE instance updates all other instances with a vector of its services, the updates are sent as bundle. Across different systems, however, this would lead to another n messages as the BASE internal mechanism could not be reused to broadcast the existence of the coordinator.

For coordination purposes, COMITY adds 2 messages per application for the registration process and 1 message for the addition/activation/removal of each alternative context configuration. Furthermore, leases were implemented that applications must renew every $100ms$ on the coordinator. This allows for the information of active applications to be kept up to date even in dynamic environments. The leases add one extra message per detection cycle to the communication overhead.

8.2. Performance Measurements

Having discussed the memory requirements and the overhead caused by coordination, this section focuses on the evaluation of the application coordination process. At first, Section 8.2.1 gives an overview of the process and analyzes its critical path. Two subprocesses which play an important role on the critical path are *interference detection* and *interference resolution*. Consequently, Section 8.2.2 evaluates the performance of the two implemented algorithms, *BasicInterferenceDetection* and *OptimizedInterferenceDetection*. Subsequently, Section 8.2.3 conducts and discusses measurement to evaluate the implemented algorithms – NO-NP, O-NP, NO-P, and O-P.

8.2.1. Critical Path

The critical path of the application coordination process defines the minimal sequence of steps which is performed in an application-coordinator interaction. Hence, the critical path determines the minimal time required for the interaction starting with a call on the coordinator and ending with a possible adaptation instruction sent to the application. In the following the single steps on the critical path are discussed and the time requirements are analyzed.

Figure 8.1 gives an overview of the entire process of application coordination. The process starts when an application registers for coordination at the coordinator (1). In

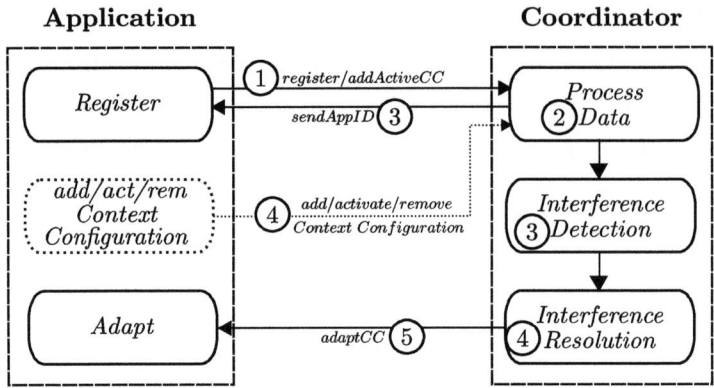

Figure 8.1.: Overview: Application Coordination Process

this process, the application provides the coordinator with its callback information and its active context configuration. Upon receipt, the coordinator processes the data. It creates an application id and adds the information contained in the context configuration to its management tables and the context model (2). As soon as the data has been processed, the coordinator sends the application id to the application (3). Furthermore, the interference detection process is triggered, if the addition of the context configuration has led to a change in the context or the set of interference specifications (3). With the provided application id, the application can now add, activate, or remove context configurations at the coordinator. Interference detection is always triggered when the context or the set of interference specifications are changed, e.g. through the activation or removal of context configurations. If one or more interferences are detected in the interference detection process, interference resolution is triggered (4). This subprocess computes the interference resolution plan and instructs pervasive applications to adapt according to the plan (5).

Analytically, the time required from (1) through (5) can be determined as shown in Equation 8.1, where $OWNC$ is the time required for a one-way network communication (1)(5), DP the time required for data processing (2), ID the time required for interference detection (3), and IR the time required for interference resolution (4).

8.2. Performance Measurements

$$T(CP) = OWNC + DP + ID + IR + OWNC \tag{8.1}$$

To obtain the values for the variables of the equation, separate measurements were conducted. At first, measurements were performed to obtain the times for $OWNC$ and DP. $OWNC$ clearly depends on the employed communication middleware, i.e. BASE. DP in turn is determined by two subprocesses implemented in the prototype. At first, the coordinator creates an application id (IDP) and subsequently adds the information held in the context configuration to the management tables (CCP). The results of the measurements are shown in Table 8.4. The parameter that was varied was the length of the context configurations, i.e. the number of attributes in the interference specification (IS) and context influences (CI). The measurements also showed that the structure of the interference specification did not have an impact on the results. Whether the interference specification consisted of a single composed context constraint containing several atomic context constraints or several composed context constraints containing a single atomic context constraint each did not make a difference.

The setup of the test scenario was as follows: The coordinator – realized as a BASE service – was executed on a desktop PC with Intel Core2Quad Q 6600 @ 2.40 GHz and 4 GB RAM running a 64 Bit Windows 7. The application – whose representative part is also realized as a BASE service – was executed on a Sony Vaio Solo U1500@1.33 GHz with 1 GB RAM running a Windows Vista Business which is comparable to contemporary smartphones. The communication was provided via LAN. The $OWNC$ was determined as half an average communication round trip time. For each setting, a number of 50 runs was performed. The obtained average time is given in Table 8.4.

Processes		$|CI/IS|$					
		1	4	9	16	25	36
$OWNC$		1.80ms	1.60ms	1.80ms	1.50ms	1.70ms	1.80ms
DP	IDP	0.50ms	0.50ms	0.45ms	0.45ms	0.45ms	0.45ms
	CCP	1.20ms	1.20ms	1.20ms	1.40ms	1.70ms	1.70ms
$Overall$		5.30ms	4.90ms	5.25ms	4.85ms	5.55ms	5.75ms

Table 8.4.: Performance Results for the Critical Path

The table shows the time required for the overall process for different sizes of context configurations $|CI/IS| = \{1, 2, 4, 9, 16, 25, 36\}$. The results indicate that required time does not vary significantly. The application required between $4.85ms$ and $5.75ms$ to register an active context configuration at the coordinator ensuring that the interferences of the application are handled in the system and getting an application id as return value. For a context configuration size of 9 for example, the one way network communication required $1.8ms$, the data processing required $0.45ms$ for the creation of an id and $1.2ms$ for processing the data contained in the context configuration. The overall time it took an application to be ensured that its interferences are detected and measures are taken to resolve them with a context configuration of 9 was $5.25ms$.

The measurement results shown in table 8.4 summarize the time required to communicate with the coordinator and to provide the coordinator with respective information. Part of the critical path, however, are the processes of interference detection ID and interference resolution IR. With respect to interference detection and resolution, the performance depends on the employed algorithms. Furthermore, since a prototypic implementation is evaluated, optimizations with respect to the implementation are conceivable. In the following, Section 8.2.2 discusses the performance of interference detection followed by the evaluation of interference resolution in Section 8.2.3.

8.2.2. Interference Detection

In order to assess the performance of interference resolution, measurements were conducted for the implementations of the *BasicInterferenceDetection* algorithm and the *OptimizedInterferenceDetection* algorithm. The evaluation of both algorithms was conducted on a Quad-Core Intel(R) Xeon(R)@2.33GHz device with 6GB RAM running a 64 Bit Windows Server Standard Edition.

For the measurements, two different scenarios were set up as follows: a number of $n = \{1, 5, 25, 50, 100, 200, 500\}$ active context configurations were added to the coordinator. The context configurations were designed such that the initial setup did not yield

8.2. Performance Measurements

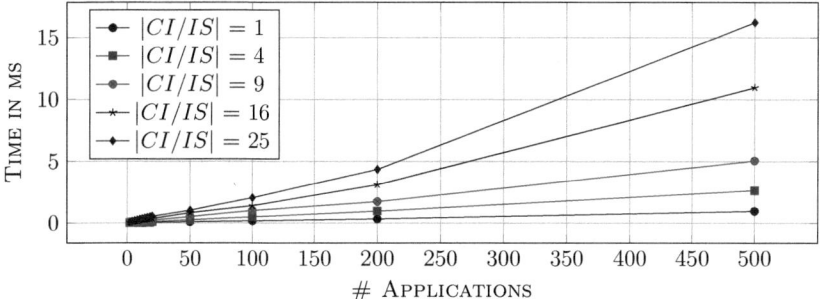

Figure 8.2.: Measurement Results for *BasicInterferenceDetection*

any interferences. After the context configurations had been added, the context was changed such that (1) one of n interference specification would be satisfied by one active context configuration or (2) 1 of the n interference specifications would be satisfied by n applications. Due to the design, the *BasicInterferenceDetection* had to evaluate all interference specifications of active context configuration, i.e. n interference specifications, for the changed context. Besides the number of active context configurations, the size of context configurations with $|CI/IS| = \{1, 4, 9, 16, 25\}$ served as a second parameter. This parameter indicates how many different context attributes were addressed in the context influences and the interference specification. Each setup was repeated 20 times.

Figure 8.2 shows the results for the *BasicInterferenceDetection* algorithm. The x-axis depicts the number of applications and thus the number of active context configurations being added to the coordinator. The y-axis shows the required time to detect the interference in milliseconds.

$$T(ID) = \#Apps \cdot |CI| \cdot |CIC| \qquad (8.2)$$

The time required for interference detection is summarized in Equation 8.2 and is determined as follows: for each application that is registered at the coordinator with an active context configuration, the active interference specification must be evaluated resulting in $\#Apps$. For each of these interference specifications, atomic context constraints with

$|CI|$ context attributes must be evaluated. If the atomic context constraint makes use of quantifiers, all candidates CIC held in the context must be considered.

$$T(ID/ID) = \#Apps \cdot |CI| \cdot |CIC| \cdot avg(CTXE) \qquad (8.3)$$

An additional factor is added – $avg(CTXE)$ as shown in Equation 8.3 – if the creation of the interference description is integrated into the interference detection process. The integration is reasonable, as it avoids a second evaluation of the interference specification. The additional factor is caused through the structure of the context model as described in Section 7.4.2. For each context attribute, the context model holds an entry for the final value and a list of entries that influence the context attribute. In case the final value satisfies an atomic context constraint, the list is parsed for all application sources that contribute to the final value. For satisfying entries, the application id and the context are added to the interference description.

The *OptimizedInterferenceDetection* algorithm was evaluated in the same setup. Recall that the optimized version only evaluates the interference specifications which could be affected by a context change. Thus, only those interference specifications are checked that reference a context attribute ctx_a, if the value of ctx_a was changed since the detection was performed last. Table 8.5 gives an overview of the times required for the optimized interference detection in comparison to the non-optimized version in milliseconds. For the subsequent discussion, the measurement results for $|CI/IS| = 9$ were selected.

The measurement results show that the optimized version reduces the required time between 12% and 20% for 1:1 interferences. For 1:n interferences, the optimized version is even able to reduce the required time up to 60%. The results also give an indication for which context change rate the coordination can still handle interference detection. For example, the coordination is able to handle about 1400 context updates a second in order to detect interferences for 50 application if 1:1 interferences must be detected.

With respect to the targeted pervasive systems, interference detection can be applied in time-critical systems. Using a room-centric approach, the execution of more than

8.2. Performance Measurements

		SETUP					
		BID 1:1	OID 1:1	Red.	BID 1:n	OID 1:n	Red.
# APPLICATIONS	2	0.0493ms	0.0451ms	-12%	0.0506ms	0.0270ms	-47%
	4	0.0670ms	0.0590ms	-12%	0.0649ms	0.0423ms	-35%
	6	0.0810ms	0.0695ms	-15%	0.0968ms	0.0544ms	-44%
	8	0.1028ms	0.0867ms	-16%	0.1251ms	0.0770ms	-39%
	10	0.1191ms	0.1016ms	-15%	0.1591ms	0.0923ms	-42%
	12	0.1418ms	0.1160ms	-19%	0.1876ms	0.1135ms	-39%
	14	0.1651ms	0.1336ms	-20%	0.2163ms	0.1289ms	-40%
	16	0.1783ms	0.1476ms	-18%	0.2508ms	0.1422ms	-43%
	18	0.2012ms	0.1619ms	-20%	0.2773ms	0.1580ms	-44%
	20	0.2231ms	0.1790ms	-20%	0.3079ms	0.1818ms	-41%
	50	0.5246ms	0.4240ms	-20%	0.7489ms	0.4162ms	-45%
	100	0.9985ms	0.8756ms	-12%	1.3645ms	0.7030ms	-50%
	200	1.7361ms	1.5278ms	-14%	2.5130ms	1.4320ms	-44%
	500	5.0591ms	4.5022ms	-12%	9.9831ms	4.0299ms	-60%

Table 8.5.: Basic vs. Optimized Interference Detection, $|CI/IS| = 9$

100 applications seems unlikely. However, even with 200 applications, the optimized interference detection is able to detect about 700 1:n interferences within one second. However, interference detection only contributes a small part to the overall time required on the critical path. As the next section shows, the task of computing an interference resolution plan is the most time consuming subprocess in the overall process of application coordination.

8.2.3. Interference Resolution Plan Computation

The goal of this section is to assess the performance of the algorithms implemented for interference resolution. As previously discussed, interference resolution consists of two subprocesses, the interference resolution plan computation and the initiation of application adaptations. While the latter constitutes the distribution of adaptation requests, the former is a complex task. In Section 5.4.2.5 an ordering heuristic was introduced and the use of pruning was suggested to realize an informed backtracking. In order to evaluate the improvements, measurements were conducted for all four variations, *no ordering - no pruning* (NO-NP), *ordering - no pruning* (O-NP), *no ordering - pruning* (NO-P), and *ordering - pruning* (O-P). In this setup, the non-intelligent backtracking (NO-NP) serves as a reference algorithm.

To test the two improvements specifically, two different test cases were set up. In both cases, the algorithms had to compute an interference resolution plan for a given interference. However, while the first test case only required applications to be adapted that are initially involved in the interference for its resolution, the second test case required the adaptation of further, uninvolved applications. In order to provide a clear discussion, the first test case is described and its results are discussed before the second test case is addressed.

Test case 1: The goal of the first test case was to assess the quality of the improvements for interferences where the adaptation of involved applications suffices to resolve the interference. The parameters were: (1) the number of applications $n = \{2, 4, 6, 8\}$ which are registered at the coordinator, (2) the number of context configurations per application $m = \{2, 4, 8\}$, where one configuration is the active one, (3) the number of context configurations per application that can resolve the interference $r = \{1, m/2\}$ and thus have an impact on the density of the solution space, and (4) the number of applications involved in the initial interference $i = \{2, n/2, n\}$. The number of attributes per context configuration was fixed to $|CI/IS| = 5$. A set of 20 runs was performed per point. The order of context configurations for each application was randomly generated in each run.

While the setup provides different variations, a setup with $m = 8$ and $i = 2$ was chosen as a representative scenario for this discussion. The choice for 8 context configurations per application was made because it provides the largest search space among the possible variations. Thus, the overall number of combinations an algorithm must evaluate in the worst case is 8^n. Furthermore, a number of 2 applications was selected as required to adapt to find a solution in order to emphasize the improvements through the ordering heuristics. Moreover, the size of the search space was varied to observe the improvements through pruning. Hence, the described setup was evaluated with $r = 1$ such that only one

8.2. Performance Measurements

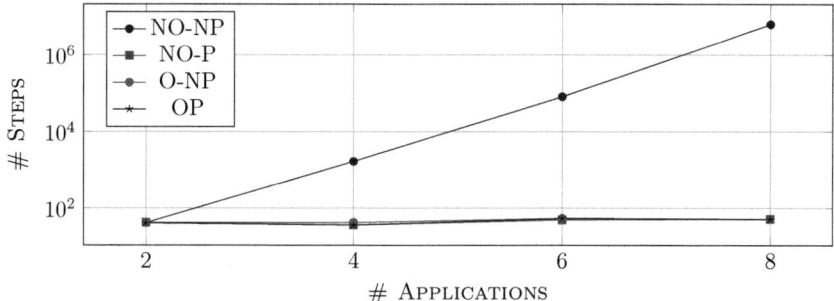

Figure 8.3.: Interference Resolution: $r = 1$, $i = 2$

out of the 8 context configurations led to the solution of the interference and $r = m/2$, i.e. half of the configurations led to a solution.

The measurement results for $n = \{2, 4, 6, 8\}$, $m = 8$, $i = 2$, and $r = 1$ are shown in Figure 8.3. The x-axis of the graph indicates the number of applications n. The y-axis depicts the average number of steps the algorithms required in order to find a solution. The figure shows that the use of either *ordering* or *pruning* or the combination of both (NO-P, O-NP, and O-P) clearly outperforms NO-NP, i.e. basic backtracking. The use of the heuristic in this scenario lets the algorithm adapt those applications first which are involved in the interference.

The complexity of all three variations lies in $O(m^i)$ with m being the number of context configurations and i being the number of interfering applications. Moreover, in this setup the complexity is independent of the number of active applications. The use of the ordering heuristic ensures that all combinations that involve the adaptation of interfering applications are evaluated before the adaptation of any non-interfering application is tried. Thus, 8^2 combinations must be evaluated in the worst case. If pruning is combined with the ordering heuristic, the effects of pruning are hardly visible. This is due to the fact that the ordering of the matrix reduces the pruning potential to a minimum.

The measurement results for $n = \{2, 4, 6, 8\}$, $m = 8$, $i = 2$, and $r = 4$ are shown in Figure 8.4. The difference in comparison to the previous setup is the increased density of the solution space. In this setup, every other of an application's context configurations led

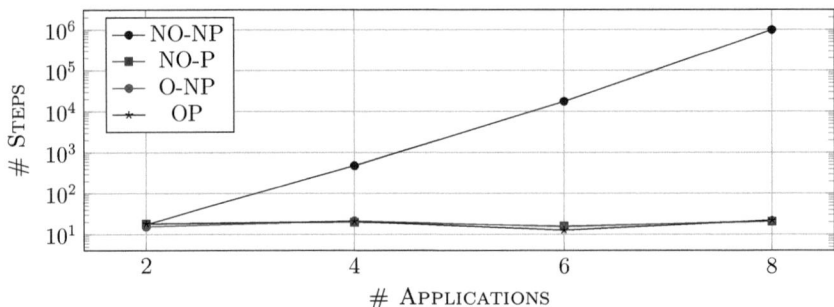

Figure 8.4.: Interference Resolution:: $r = m/2$, $i = 2$

to a solution of the interference. Overall, the graph shows the same tendency as the graph in Figure 8.3. O-NP, NO-P, and O-P clearly outperform NO-NP. Due to the choice of r, however, solutions are more frequent than in the first setup. Hence, the determination of a solution requires less steps.

In order to compare the actual number of steps, Table 8.6 gives a numeric overview of the results shown in Figure 8.3 and 8.4. Furthermore, Table 8.7 shows evaluation results for a number of $m = 4$ context configurations per application. While $m = 8$ supported a better exposition of the improvements through ordering and pruning, 4 context configurations seem to be more likely in practice. An application may have a number of different functional configurations. However, the context configurations of different functional configurations may be identical. As an example, a music application may have several functional configurations which employ different output resources. Even though the output resources may differ, the context interaction stays the same if they all output music to the environment. In addition to the average number of steps that were required to find a solution, the table also shows the taken time in milliseconds.

The results in both tables show that NO-NP is not applicable for interference resolution in time-critical pervasive systems. In a setup for 8 applications with 4 context configurations each and a dense distribution of solutions in the search space, NO-NP takes about 521 milliseconds to find a solution. In contrast, NO-P, O-NP, and OP perform similarly and solve the interference in between $0.5ms$ and $3.9ms$. The measured times also indicate

8.2. Performance Measurements

		\multicolumn{2}{c}{$m=4, r=1$}	\multicolumn{2}{c}{$m=4, r=m/2$}
		Steps	Time	Steps	Time
NO-NP	2	11.8	0.9203ms	7.8	1.5428ms
NO-NP	4	131.1	3.8409ms	91.9	2.9162ms
NO-NP	6	636.4	27.4153ms	634.7	26.9436ms
NO-NP	8	14190	855.4604ms	8827.9	521.1618ms
NO-P	2	11.5	2.6971ms	8.1	3.879ms
NO-P	4	13.5	1.1856ms	8.5	0.7690ms
NO-P	6	11.5	0.6630ms	8	0.8222ms
NO-P	8	12	0.8917ms	8.2	0.6330ms
O-NP	2	11.5	0.8550ms	8.1	0.6528ms
O-NP	4	13.2	0.4278ms	8.5	0.3203ms
O-NP	6	12.1	0.5681ms	7.7	0.3744ms
O-NP	8	12	0.7757ms	8.5	0.5640ms
O-P	2	11.5	2.7354ms	8.4	4.2097ms
O-P	4	12.3	1.0428ms	8.8	07619ms
O-P	6	11.2	0.6289ms	8	0.8189ms
O-P	8	13.5	0.9729ms	8.8	0.6367ms

Table 8.6.: Test Case 1: Required Steps and Time, $m=4$

		\multicolumn{2}{c}{$m=8, r=1$}	\multicolumn{2}{c}{$m=8, r=1$}
		Steps	Time	Steps	Time
NO-NP	2	41.2	1.1056ms	17.4	0.9084ms
NO-NP	4	1660.8	50.0728ms	475.6	13.7538ms
NO-NP	6	80456	3448.6ms	17566.5	745.7630ms
NO-NP	8	6275075	364537ms	988300	56808ms
NO-P	2	41.8	2.1569ms	19.5	2.2915ms
NO-P	4	40.3	1.6877ms	17.8	1.1648ms
NO-P	6	52.6	2.8751ms	15.4	0.8732ms
NO-P	8	50.6	3.4173ms	21.3	1.5162ms
O-NP	2	42.5	1.2114ms	15.3	0.8159ms
O-NP	4	42.4	1.3150ms	21.3	0.6657ms
O-NP	6	54	2.4374ms	15.4	0.7340ms
O-NP	8	52	3.2630ms	21.3	1.3645ms
O-P	2	43.9	2.2605ms	18.8	2.3092ms
O-P	4	41.7	1.6455ms	19.9	1.3297ms
O-P	6	48.8	2.2205ms	16.1	0.8754ms
O-P	8	53.4	3.5158ms	17.1	1.1936ms

Table 8.7.: Test Case 1: Required Steps and Time, $m=8$

that the algorithms do not come close to their limits. However, as previously discussed, the complexity for O-NP and O-P is dependent on the number of context configurations and the number of interfering applications. As a consequence, the performance will not change with an increasing number of applications. The time requirement will change if the number of context configurations is changed – which does not seem reasonable as discussed earlier – or more applications are involved in the initial interference and need to be adapted.

While the results suggest that the algorithms can be employed to detect interferences in pervasive systems without any reservations, the scenario in test case 1 does not represent typical interferences. In practice, the number of applications which need to be adapted to resolve an interference is not known until a solution is found. For this purpose, a second test case was set up in which initially uninvolved applications need to be adapted in addition to interfering applications to resolve the interference.

		$m=4, r=1$		$m=4, r=1$	
		Steps	Time	Steps	Time
NO-P	4	135.5	$0.008s$	95.1	$0.009s$
	6	1530	$0.091s$	1825	$0.102s$
	8	41448	$3.6335s$	22704	$1.847s$
	10	443894.8	$51.852s$	567161	$41.360s$
O-P	4	163.4	$0.009s$	121.1	$0.013s$
	6	2081	$0.127s$	1883.5	$0.105s$
	8	45927	$3.9968s$	35817.12	$2.9080s$
	10	620875	$73.23s$	550156	$59.1857s$

Table 8.8.: Test Case 2: Required Steps and Time, $m=4$

Test case 2: The goal of the second test case was to assess the quality of the use of ordering and pruning for interferences where the adaptation of initially involved applications does not suffice. As in the first test case, the parameters were: (1) the number of applications $n = \{2, 4, 6, 8\}$ which are registered at the coordinator, (2) the number of context configurations per application $m = \{2, 4, 8\}$ where one configuration is the active one, (3) the number of context configurations per application that can resolve the interference $r = \{1, m/2\}$ and thus have an impact on the density of the solution space, and (4) the number of applications involved in the initial interference $i = \{2, n/2, n\}$. In

8.2. Performance Measurements

addition, (5) the number of applications that need to be adapted with $a = \{n/2, n\}$ was added as parameter. The number of attributes per context configuration was fixed to $|CI/IS| = 5$.

		$m = 8, r = 1$		$m = 8, r = 1$	
		Steps	Time	Steps	Time
NO-P	4	1304	0.050s	921.3	0.036s
NO-P	6	81238	5.129s	48843	2.834s
NO-P	8	6291376	595.603s	4296380	361.276s
O-P	4	2066.1	0.082s	1262.9	0.058s
O-P	6	1185426	7.574s	49088	2.839s
O-P	8	7562447	713.744s	3838073.5	320.682s

Table 8.9.: Test Case 2: Required Steps and Time, $m = 8$

For test case 2, the results showed that the only viable variations of the resolution algorithm are the ones that use *pruning*, i.e. NO-P and O-P. As further interferences are detected while searching for an interference resolution plan, the ordering heuristic does not improve the performance. In contrast, in the combination with pruning, the ordering heuristic reduces the pruning potential. The reason for that is shown in Figures 8.5(a) and 8.5(b). The use of the ordering heuristic places the applications which are initially involved in the interference to the right of the input matrix. This means that these applications are adapted first in order to find a solution. However, the way pruning works, only the last application can be adapted which is part of the interference. In Figure 8.5(a), the interfering application that can be adapted is application 1. Since application 1 is the last application in the matrix, pruning is not possible. In contrast, if applications were ordered differently, i.e. without the use of the ordering heuristic, pruning is likely to have more potential. Figure 8.5(b) shows the same context configuration as Figure 8.5(a) but with permutated application positions.

Tables 8.8 and 8.9 state the performance of NOP and OP for 4 and 8 context configurations respectively. The parameters in this test were set to: $m = 4, 8$, $r = 1, m/2$, $i = 2$, and $a = n$, respectively. In this very complex setting, the best-performing NOP takes 0.009s, 0.102s, 1.847s, and 41.360s for finding a resolution in a system with 4, 6, 8, and 10 applications and 4 context configurations.

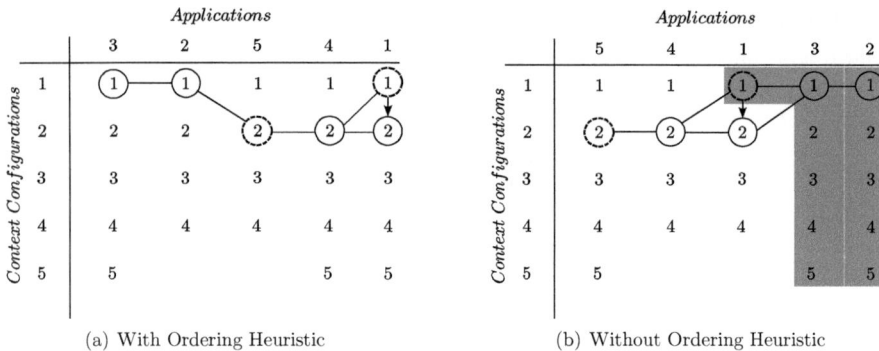

Figure 8.5.: Ordering vs. Non-Ordering

In summary, the use of NO-P has proven to be the best option for the computation of an interference resolution plan. For interferences which exclusively require those applications to be adapted that are initially involved in the interference, O-NP, NO-P, and O-P are all comparable with respect to their performance. For interferences, which require the adaptation of further, uninvolved applications for a resolution, NO-P outperforms all other variations. However, the use of NO-P is still limited, especially in time-critical systems. As an example, the algorithm requires about $40s$ for 10 applications with 4 context configurations and large solution space to find an interference resolution plan. Adding the time required for communication and interference detection, this may add up to about $45s$ in which the interference persists and the experience of a seamless functionality provision is disturbed.

In summary, this chapter evaluated the prototype and its implemented concepts. The analysis of the memory requirements showed that the size of COMITY is dependent on the number of managed context configurations and their memory requirements. Furthermore, performance measurements with respect to the critical path were conducted. The single steps of the path were analyzed and the results showed that the communication with the coordinator – excluding the processes of interference detection and resolution – takes about $5ms$-$6ms$ using BASE as communication middleware. Subsequently, the algorithms for

8.2. Performance Measurements

interference detection and resolution were evaluated. While the results indicate that the optimized interference detection is suitable for time-critical pervasive systems, interference resolution proves to be the bottleneck regarding the application coordination process. In order to be applicable in time-critical systems, further improvements, considering the performance of interference resolution, are required.

9. Conclusion and Outlook

This chapter summarizes the contents of this thesis and provides an outlook on future work.

9.1. Conclusion

The extrapolation of the current trends in pervasive computing suggests that future human environments will be managed by a multitude of different pervasive systems. In order to provide functionality, each of these systems will execute pervasive applications. A major characteristic of such applications is their context-interactivity. On one hand, pervasive applications are aware of their context and can adapt themselves if the context changes. On the other hand, pervasive applications are able to influence and change the context. This can be done implicitly as a side effect of employed resources or explicitly through the use of respective actuators. If multiple applications are executed in the same physical space, problems are likely to occur. These problems can be reduced to the fact that applications which are executed in the same physical environment share and interact with a common context. As a consequence, they are directly related with each other as an application may change the context other applications depend on.

The described problem has been defined as an interference in this thesis. An interference is an application-produced context that impairs the functionality provision of another application. In order to show that interferences is a problem class likely to occur between pervasive applications, an overview of existing approaches has been given. The overview shows that the majority of the discussed approaches interact with their context and thus are likely to interfere with each other.

In order to handle interferences between applications across different systems, an application coordination framework has been presented. The framework is subject to three major design decisions. Firstly, the framework realizes a cross-system coordination layer to allow interference management across different systems. Secondly, it supports the integration of arbitrary application systems through the realization and provision of active and alternative context configurations and the implementation of an adaptation interface. The context configuration defines the interaction of the application in its current and alternative functional configuration. The first part of the context configuration is the interference specification which defines those context states which the application considers to be an interference, using monadic predicate logic. The second part are the context influences which describe how the application influences the context in the functional configuration. Finally, the framework provides a generic interface to enable the use of different resolution strategies allowing a customization of the framework to the needs of different pervasive systems.

The management of interferences is achieved through their automatic detection and resolution at runtime. For interference detection, the framework requires the active context configuration of each application in the pervasive system. Based on that information and a context model, interferences are automatically detected. For interference resolution, the framework makes use of the alternative context configurations provided by applications. It computes an interference resolution plan by selecting a context configuration for each application such that the pervasive system is interference free. Once a plan has been obtained, each application is instructed to instantiate a functional configuration that complies with the selected context configuration.

The analysis of the interference resolution plan computation and its modeling as a constraint satisfaction problem showed that the problem is NP-complete. As a consequence, any algorithm that solves a constraint satisfaction problem can be employed to compute an interference resolution plan. For this purpose, different algorithm classes were discussed and two informed backtracking approaches which exploit the specific structure of interferences have been introduced.

For a practical realization of the framework the component deployment in pervasive systems and the point in time when data must be exchanged has been analyzed. Furthermore, the concepts are implemented in a prototype. To assess the prototypical implementation and the underlying concepts, several measurements are conducted to evaluate them. The measurements show that with respect to the managed data, typical devices in pervasive systems, such as smartphones, are resourceful enough to coordinate up to 100 applications. Considering required tasks, the process of interference detection is performable by typical devices by all means. However, the process of interference resolution plan computation clearly constitutes the bottleneck in the application coordination process. With 10 applications with 4 context configurations, the best variation of informed backtracking required about 41 seconds.

9.2. Outlook

The application coordination framework presented in this thesis provides a solid basis to manage interferences in pervasive systems. However, this research reveals several worthwhile future directions to be explored.

Firstly, the framework could be extended in the sense that it realizes a cooperation of applications through coordination. At present, applications in different pervasive systems coexist. They do not interact with each other nor do they make use of each other's functionality. The current state of the presented framework realizes measures to maintain this state of application coexistence. In case an interference occurs, the framework automatically detects the interference and takes measures to resolve the context-based interconnection of applications. In order to make use of synergistic effects, the framework could support the cooperation of applications in different systems. Instead of defining interference specifications, applications could define goals they want to achieve but which require further support. This could enable the framework to determine the actions and activities of multiple applications in order to achieve a common goal.

Secondly, concepts could be developed to support users with respect to the creation of interference specifications. Users could define a number of interference specifications to ensure that undesired situations are handled as quickly as possible. For this purpose, a first step towards a user-interface to support the creation of interference specifications has been presented [TSB06].

Thirdly, further resolution strategies could be developed. In this thesis, four variations of a backtracking-based algorithm were analyzed and evaluated. The evaluation showed that especially for interferences that require the adaptation of initially uninvolved applications for a resolution, the proposed algorithms are hardly employable in time-critical systems. For this purpose, further resolution strategies could be developed that, for example, consider the pausing of applications for a resolution.

Lastly, the coordination framework could be provided with a proactive component. At present, the framework detects interferences when they actually happen. Based on the context configurations it then computes a resolution plan for the interference. A proactive component could detect potential interferences and compute respective resolutions before the interference actually happens. Hence, in case the predicted interference happens, a resolution is already available. The proactive coordination also promises a reduction in the overall time required for the application coordination process as the computation of an interference resolution plan is preponed.

Bibliography

[AAH+97] Gregory D. Abowd, Christopher G. Atkeson, Jason Hong, Sue Long, Rob Kooper, and Mike Pinkerton. Cyberguide: A Mobile Context-Aware Tour Guide. *Wireless Networks - Special Issue: Mobile Computing and Networking*, 3(5):421–433, 1997.

[AKM06] Ibrahim Armac, Michael Kirchhof, and Liviana Manolescu. Modeling and Analysis of Functionality in eHome Systems: Dynamic Rule-based Conflict Detection. In *Proceedings of the 13th annual IEEE International Symposium and Workshop on Engineering of Computer Based systems*, 2006.

[Bar05] Jakob E. Bardram. The Java Context Awareness Framework (JCAF) - A Service Infrastructure and Programming Framework for Context-Aware Applications. In *Proceedings of the 3rd International Conference on Pervasive Computing*, 2005.

[BBG+00] Guruduth Banavar, James Beck, Eugene Gluzberg, Jonathan Munson, Jeremy B. Sussman, and Deborra J. Zukowski. Challenges: An Application Model for Pervasive Computing. In *Proceedings of the 6th Annual International Conference on Mobile Computing and Networking*, 2000.

[BBR02] Martin Bauer, Christian Becker, and Kurt Rothermel. Location Models from the Perspective of Context-Aware Applications and Mobile Ad Hoc Networks. *Personal and Ubiquitous Computing*, 6(5-6), 2002.

[BC04] Gregory Biegel and Vinny Cahill. A Framework for Developing Mobile,

Context-Aware Applications. In *Proceedings of the 2nd IEEE International Conference on Pervasive Computing and Communications*, 2004.

[BCRZ09] Manfred Bortenschlager, Gabriella Castelli, Alberto Rosi, and Franco Zambonelli. A Context-Sensitive Infrastructure for Coordinating Agents in Ubiquitous Environments. *Multiagent Grid Systems – Engineering Environments in Multiagent Systems*, 5:1–18, 2009.

[BDR07] Matthias Baldaufs, Schahram Dustdar, and Florian Rosenberg. A Survey on Context-Aware Systems. *International Journal of Ad Hoc and Ubiquitous Computing*, 2(4):263–277, 2007.

[Ben96] Hachemi Bennaceur. The Satisfiability Problem Regarded as a Constraint Satisfaction Problem. In *Proceedings of the 12th European Conference on Artificial Intelligence*, 1996.

[BG02] Jenna Burrell and Geri K. Gay. E-graffiti: Evaluating Real-World Use of a Context-Aware System. *Interacting with Computers*, 14(4):301–312, 2002.

[BHSR04] Christian Becker, Marcus Handte, Gregor Schiele, and Kurt Rothermel. PCOM - A Component System for Pervasive Computing. In *Proceedings of the 2nd IEEE International Conference on Pervasive Computing and Communications*, 2004.

[BK01] John Barton and Tim Kindberg. The Cooltown User Experience. Tech Report: HPL-2001-22. Technical report, HP Labs, 2001.

[BKL01] Prithwish Basu, Naved Khan, and Thomas D.C. Little. A Mobility Based Metric for Clustering in Mobile Ad Hoc Networks. In *Proceedings of the International Workshop on Wireless Networks and Mobile Computing*, 2001.

[BKZD04] Michael Beigl, Albert Krohn, Tobias Zimmer, and Christian Decker. Typical sensors needed in ubiquitous and pervasive computing. In *Proceedings of the 1st International Workshop on Networked Sensing Systems*, 2004.

Bibliography

[Blu] Specification Bluetooth. https://www.bluetooth.org/Technical/Specifications/adopted.htm. Core Version 4.0, accessed 30.09.2012.

[BMV10] Carlo Bertolli, Gabriele Mencagli, and Marco Vanneschi. A cost model for autonomic reconfigurations in high-performance pervasive applications. In *Proceedings of the 4th ACM International Workshop on Context-Awareness for Self-Managing Systems*, 2010.

[Bor06] Manfred Bortenschlager. HUG CorA How to Use a Generic Coordination Architecture in Pervasive System Development. In *Adjunct Proceedings of the 4th International Conference on Pervasive Computing*, 2006.

[BR75] James R. Bitner and Edward M. Reingold. Backtrack Programming Techniques. *Communications ACM*, 18(11):651–656, 1975.

[BRK06] Manfred Bortenschlager, Sigi Reich, and Gabriele Kotsis. A Generic Coordination Architecture as an Enabler for Mobile Collaborative Applications. In *Proceedings of the 15th IEEE International Workshops on Enabling Technologies: Infrastructure for Collaborative Enterprises*, 2006.

[BSGR03] Christian Becker, Gregor Schiele, Holger Gubbels, and Kurt Rothermel. BASE – A Micro-broker-based Middleware For Pervasive Computing. In *Proceedings of the IEEE International Conference on Pervasive Computing and Communications*, 2003.

[BSI06] Federal Office for Information Security BSI. *Pervasive Computing: Trends and Impacts*. SecuMedia Verlags-GmbH, 2006.

[BZD02] Michael Beigl, Tobias Zimmer, and Christian Decker. A Location Model for Communicating and Processing of Context. *Personal Ubiquitous Computing*, 6(5-6):341–357, 2002.

[CAMCM05] Shiva Chetan, Jalal Al-Muhtadi, Roy Campbell, and M. Dennis Mickunas. Mobile Gaia: A Middleware for Ad-Hoc Pervasive Computing. In

Proceedings of the 2nd IEEE Consumer Communications and Networking Conference, 2005.

[CCM+05] Paolo Costa, Geoff Coulson, Cecilia Mascolo, Gian Pietro Picco, and Stefanos Zachariadis. The RUNES Middleware: A Reconfigurable Component-Based Approach to Networked Embedded Systems. In *Proceedings of the 16th Annual IEEE International Symposium on Personal Indoor and Mobile Radio Communications*, 2005.

[CDM+00] Keith Cheverst, Nigel Davies, Keith Mitchell, Adrian Friday, and Christos Efstratiou. Developing a Context-Aware Electronic Tourist Guide: Some Issues and Experiences. In *Proceedings of the SIGCHI Conference on Human Factors in Computing Systems*, 2000.

[CEM03] Licia Capra, Wolfgang Emmerich, and Cecilia Mascolo. CARISMA: Context-Aware Reflective mIddleware System for Mobile Applications. *IEEE Transactions on Software Engineering*, 29(10):929–945, 2003.

[CFJ03] Harry Chen, Tim Finin, and Anupam Joshi. An Ontology for Context-Aware Pervasive Computing Environments. *Special Issue on Ontologies for Distributed Systems, Knowledge Engineering Review*, 18:197–207, 2003.

[Chu36] Alonzo Church. A Note on the Entscheidungsproblem. *Journal of Symbolic Logic*, 1(1):40–41, 1936.

[CJP87] Jr. Charles J. Petrie. Revised Dependency-Directed Backtracking for Default Reasoning. In *Proceedings of the 6th National Conference on Artificial Intelligence*, 1987.

[CLK04] Guanling Chen, Ming Li, and David Kotz. Design and Implementation of a Large-Scale Context Fusion Network. In *Proceedings of the 1st Annual International Conference on Mobile and Ubiquitous Systems: Networking and Services*, 2004.

Bibliography

[Coo71]   Stephen A. Cook. The Complexity of Theorem-Proving Procedures. In *Proceedings of the 3rd Annual ACM Symposium on Theory of Computing*, 1971.

[Coo89]   Martin C. Cooper. An Optimal K-Consistency Algorithm. *Artificial Intelligence*, 41(1):89–95, 1989.

[Cor]   HTC Corporation. HTC One X+ Specification. http://www.htc.com/www/smartphones/htc-one-x-plus/#specs. accessed 20.10.2012.

[CPFJ04]   Harry Chen, Filip Perich, Tim Finin, and Anupam Joshi. SOUPA: Standard Ontology for Ubiquitous and Pervasive Applications. In *Proceedings the 1st Annual International Conference on Mobile and Ubiquitous Systems: Networking and Services*, 2004.

[CSW05]   Yoosoo Oh Choonsung Shin and Woontack Woo. History-Based Conflict Management for Multi-Users and Multi-Services. In *Proceedings of the 1st Workshop on Context Modeling and Decision Support*, 2005.

[Dey01]   Anind K. Dey. Understanding and Using Context. *Personal Ubiquitous Computing*, 5(1):4–7, 2001.

[DF98]   Rina Dechter and Daniel Frost. Backtracking Algorithms for Constraint Satisfaction Problems - A Tutorial Survey. Technical report, University of California, Irvine, 1998.

[DGM+11]   Oleg Davidyuk, Ekaterina Gilman, Iván Sánchez Milara, Jussi Mäkipelto, Mikko Pyykkönen, and Jukka Riekki. iCompose: Context-Aware Physical User Interface for Application Composition. *Central European Journal of Computer Science*, 1(4):442–465, 2011.

[DGV03]   Philippe Debaty, Patrick Goddi, and Alex Vorbau. Integrating the Physical World With the Web to Enable Context-Enhanced Mobile Services. *Mobile Networks and Applications*, 10:385–394, 2003.

[DHH07]   Anusuriya Devaraju, Simon Hoh, and Michael Hartley. A Context Gathering Framework for Context-Aware Mobile Solutions. In *Proceedings of the 4th International Conference on Mobile Technology, Applications, and Systems*, 2007.

[DIK02]   Nicole Dunlop, Jadwiga Indulska, and Raymond Kerry. Dynamic Conflict Detection in Policy-Based Management Systems. In *Proceedings of the 6th International Enterprise Distributed Object Computing Conference*, 2002.

[Doy79]   Jon Doyle. A Truth Maintenance System. *Artificial Intelligence*, 12:231–272, 1979.

[EPS+01]   Fredrik Espinoza, Per Persson, Anna Sandin, Hanna Nyström, Elenor Cacciatore, and Markus Bylund. Geonotes: Social and Navigational Aspects of Location-Based Information Systems. In *Proceedings of the 3rd International Conference on Ubiquitous Computing*, 2001.

[EWB87]   Anthony Ephremides, Jeffrey E. Wieselthier, and Dennis J. Baker. A Design Concept for Reliable Mobile Radio Networks with Frequency Hopping Signaling. *Proceedings of IEEE*, 75(1):56–73, 1987.

[FHMO04]   Alois Ferscha, Manfred Hechinger, Rene Mayrhofer, and Roy Oberhauser. A Light-Weight Component Model for Peer-to-Peer Applications. In *Proceedings of the 24th International Conference on Distributed Computing Systems Workshops*, 2004.

[Fra10]   Jakob Frankenbach. Design and Realisation of a Context Model for Pervasive Computing Environments, 2010. Bachelor Thesis, Chair of Information Systems II, University of Mannheim, Germany.

[Fre88]   Eugene C. Freuder. Backtrack-Free and Backtrack-Bounded Search. In *Search in Artificial Intelligence*, pages 343–369. Springer-Verlag, 1988.

Bibliography

[Gas79] John Gary Gaschnig. *Performance Measurement and Analysis of Certain Search Algorithms*. PhD thesis, Carnegie Mellon University, 1979.

[GDH+01] Robert Grimm, Janet Davis, Ben Hendrickson, Eric Lemar, Adam Macbeth, Steven Swanson, Tom Anderson, Brian Bershad, Gaetano Borriello, Steven Gribble, and David Wetherall. Programming for Pervasive Computing Environments. In *Proceedings of the 18th ACM Symposium on Operating Systems Principle*, 2001.

[GPS] Website GPS. http://www.gps.gov. accessed 30.09.2012.

[GPZW04] Tao Gu, Hung Keng Pung, Da Qing Zhang, and Xiao Hang Wang. A Middleware for Building Context-Aware Mobile Services. In *Proceedings of IEEE Vehicular Technology Conference*, 2004.

[Gro07] Object Management Group. OMG Unified Modeling Language (OMG UML), Infrastructure, v2.1.2. Technical report, Object Management Group, 2007.

[Gru93] Thomas R. Gruber. A Translation Approach to Portable Ontology Specifications. *Knowledge Acquisition*, 5(2):199–220, 1993.

[GRWK09] Kurt Geihs, Roland Reichle, Michael Wagner, and Mohammad Khan. Modeling of Context-Aware Self-Adaptive Applications in Ubiquitous and Service-Oriented Environments. In *Software Engineering for Self-Adaptive Systems*, volume 5525 of *Lecture Notes in Computer Science*, pages 146–163. Springer Berlin / Heidelberg, 2009.

[GSSS02] David Garlan, Dan Siewiorek, Asim Smailagic, and Peter Steenkiste. Project Aura: Toward Distraction-Free Pervasive Computing. *IEEE Pervasive Computing*, 1(2):22–31, 2002.

[Gu89] Jun Gu. *Parallel Algorithms and Architectures for Very Fast AI Search*. PhD thesis, University of Utah, 1989.

[HAM+06]   Md. Kamrul Hasan, Kim Anh, Lenin Mehedy, Young-Koo Lee, and Sungyoung Lee. Conflict Resolution and Preference Learning in Ubiquitous Environment. In *Proceedings of the International Conference on Intelligent Computing*, 2006.

[HE80]   Robert M. Haralick and Gordon L. Elliot. Increasing Tree Search Efficiency for Constraint Satisfaction Problems. *Artificial Intelligence*, 14(3):263–313, 1980.

[HHM09]   Muhammad Haroon, Marcus Handte, and Pedro Jose Marron. Generic Role Assignment: A Uniform Middleware Abstraction for Configuration of Pervasive Systems. In *Proceedings of the 7th Annual IEEE International Conference on Pervasive Computing and Communications*, 2009.

[HHS+02]   Andy Harter, Andy Hopper, Pete Steggles, Andy Ward, and Paul Webster. The Anatomy of a Context-Aware Application. *Wireless Networks*, 8(2/3):187–197, 2002.

[HIMB05]   Karen Henricksen, Jadwiga Indulska, Ted McFadden, and Sasitharan Balasubramaniam. Middleware for Distributed Context-Aware Systems. In *Proceedings of OTM Conferences (1)*, 2005.

[HME+06]   Pablo A. Haya, Germán Montoro, Abraham Esquivel, Manuel García-Herranz, and Xavier Alamán. A Mechanism for Solving Conflicts in Ambient Intelligent Environments. *Journal of Universal Computer Science*, 12(3):284–296, 2006.

[HPL+03]   Thomas Hofer, Mario Pichler, Gerhard Leonhartsberger, Josef Altmann, and Werner Retschitzegger. Context-Awareness on Mobile Devices - the Hydrogen Approach. In *Proceedings of the 36th Annual Hawaii International Conference on System Sciences*, 2003.

[HRKD08]   Klaus Herrmann, Kurt Rothermel, Gerd Kortuem, and Naranker Dulay.

Adaptable Pervasive Flows - An Emerging Technology for Pervasive Adaptation. In *Proceedings of the 2nd IEEE International Conference on Self-Adaptive and Self-Organizing Systems Workshops*, 2008.

[JCL11] Henner Jakob, Charles Consel, and Nicolas Loriant. Architecturing Conflict Handling of Pervasive Computing Resources. In *Proceedings of the 11th IFIP WG 6.1 International Conference on Distributed Applications and Interoperable Systems*, 2011.

[JF02] Brad Johanson and Armando Fox. The Event Heap: A Coordination Infrastructure for Interactive Workspaces. In *Proceedings of the 4th IEEE Workshop on Mobile Computing Systems and Applications*, 2002.

[JS03] Glenn Judd and Peter Steenkiste. Providing Contextual Information to Pervasive Computing Applications. In *Proceedings of the IEEE International Conference on Pervasive Computing and Communications*, 2003.

[KMK+03] Panu Korpipää, Jani Mantyjarvi, Juha Kela, Heikki Keranen, and Esko-Juhani Malm. Managing Context Information in Mobile Devices. *IEEE Pervasive Computing*, 2(3):42–51, 2003.

[KMW03] Mario Kolberg, Evan H. Magill, and Michael Wilson. Compatibility Issues Between Services Supporting Networked Appliances. *Communications Magazine, IEEE*, 41(11):136–147, 2003.

[Kum92] Vipin Kumar. Algorithms for Constraint Satisfaction Problems: A Survey. *AI Magazine*, 13(1):32–44, 1992.

[LPP+07] Haining Lee, Jaeil Park, Peom Park, Myungchul Jung, and Dongmin Shin. Dynamic Conflict Detection and Resolution in a Human-Centered Ubiquitous Environment. In *Proceedings of the 4th International Conference on Universal Access in Human-Computer Interaction: Ambient Interaction*, 2007.

[Löw31]   Leopold Löwenheim. *A Source Book in Mathematical Logic*, chapter On possibilities in the calculus of relatives, pages 228–251. Harvard University Press, 1879-1931.

[Mac77]   Alan K. Mackworth. Consistency in Networks of Relations. *Artificial Intelligence*, 8:99–118, 1977.

[MAJ07]   Amirreza Masoumzadeh, Morteza Amini, and Rasool Jalili. Conflict Detection and Resolution in Context-Aware Authorization. In *Proceedings of the 21st International Conference on Advanced Information Networking and Applications Workshops*, 2007.

[MD06]   Ricardo Morla and Nigel Davies. A Framework for Describing Interference in Ubiquitous Computing Environments. In *Proceedings of the 4th IEEE International Conference on Pervasive Computing and Communications Workshops*, 2006.

[MD07]   Ricardo Morla and Nigel Davies. Informing the Design of User Studies on Conceptual Interference Frameworks. In *Proceedings of the 21st International Conference on Advanced Information Networking and Applications Workshops*, 2007.

[MH86]   Roger Mohr and Thomas C. Henderson. Arc and Path Consistency Revisited. *Artificial Intelligence*, 28(2):225–233, 1986.

[MJPL92]   Steven Minton, Mark D. Johnston, Andrew B. Philips, and Philip Laird. Minimizing Conflicts: A Heuristic Repair Method for Constraint Satisfaction and Scheduling Problems. *Artificial Intelligence*, 58(1-3):161–205, 1992.

[Mor93]   Paul Morris. The Breakout Method for Escaping From Local Minima. In *Proceedings of the 11th National Conference on Artificial Intelligence*, 1993.

[MSS+10]   Verena Majuntke, Gregor Schiele, Kai Spohrer, Marcus Handte, and Christian Becker. A Coordination Framework for Pervasive Applications in Multi-

Bibliography

User Environments. In *Proceedings of the Sixth International Conference on Intelligent Environments*, 2010.

[MV03] Shivajit Mohapatra and Nalini Venkatasubramanian. PARM : Power Aware Reconfigurable Middleware. In *Proceedings of the 23rd International Conference on Distributed Computing Systems*, 2003.

[OSWS06] Friederike Otto, Choonsung Shin, Woontack Woo, and Albrecht Schmidt. A User Survey on: How to Deal with Conflicts Resulting from Individual Input Devices in Context-Aware Environments. In *Adjunct Proceedings of the 4th International Conference on Pervasive Computing*, 2006.

[Pas97] Jason Pascoe. The Stick-e Note Architecture: Extending the Interface Beyond the User. In *Proceedings of the 2nd International Conference on Intelligent User Interfaces*, 1997.

[PJKF03] Shankar R. Ponnekanti, Brad Johanson, Emre Kiciman, and Armando Fox. Portability, Extensibility and Robustness in iROS. In *Proceedings of the 1st IEEE International Conference on Pervasive Computing and Communications*, 2003.

[PLF$^+$01] Shankar R. Ponnekanti, Brian Lee, Armando Fox, Terry Winograd, and Pat Hanrahan. Icrafter : A Service Framework for Ubiquitous Computing Environments. In *Proceedings of the 3rd International Conference on Ubiquitous Computing*, 2001.

[PLH05] Insuk Park, Dongman Lee, and Soon J. Hyun. A Dynamic Context-Conflict Management Scheme for Group-Aware Ubiquitous Computing Environments. In *Proceedings of the 29th Annual International Computer Software and Applications Conference*, 2005.

[PPS$^+$08] Justin Mazzola Paluska, Hubert Pham, Umar Saif, Grace Chau, Chris Terman, and Steve Ward. Structured Decomposition of Adaptive Applications. *Pervasive Mobile Computing*, 4(6):791–806, 2008.

[Pro93]   Patrick Prosser. Hybrid Algorithms for the Constraint Satisfaction Problem. *Computational Intelligence*, 9:268–299, 1993.

[RC01]   Manuel Roman and Roy H. Campbell. Unified Object Bus: Providing Support for Dynamic Management of Heterogeneous Components. Technical report, University of Illinois at Urbana-Champaign Champaign, 2001.

[RC03]   Anand Ranganathan and Roy H. Campbell. An Infrastructure for Context-Awareness Based on First Order Logic. *Personal Ubiquitous Computing*, 7(6):353–364, 2003.

[RCAM+05]   Anand Ranganathan, Shiva Chetan, Jalal Al-Muhtadi, Roy H. Campbell, and M. Dennis Mickunas. Olympus: A High-Level Programming Model for Pervasive Computing Environments. In *Proceedings of the 3rd IEEE International Conference on Pervasive Computing and Communications*, 2005.

[RHC+02]   Manuel Román, Christopher Hess, Renato Cerqueira, Anand Ranganathan, Roy H. Campbell, and Klara Nahrstedt. A Middleware Infrastructure for Active Spaces. *IEEE Pervasive Computing*, 1(4):74–83, 2002.

[RN03]   Stuart J. Russell and Peter Norvig. *Artificial Intelligence: A Modern Approach*. Pearson Education, 2nd edition, 2003.

[Sat01]   Mahadev Satyanarayanan. Pervasive Computing: Vision and Challenges. *IEEE Personal Communications*, 8:10–17, 2001.

[Sat05]   Ichiro Satoh. A Location Model for Pervasive Computing Environments. In *Proceedings of the 3rd IEEE International Conference on Pervasive Computing and Communications*, 2005.

[SAW94]   Bill Schilit, Norman Adams, and Roy Want. Context-Aware Computing Applications. In *Proceedings of the 1994 First Workshop on Mobile Computing Systems and Applications*, 1994.

Bibliography

[Sch07] Gregor Schiele. *System Support for Spontaneous Pervasive Computing Environments*. PhD thesis, Universität Stuttgart, 2007.

[SDA99] Daniel Salber, Anind K. Dey, and Gregory D. Abowd. The Context Toolkit: Aiding the Development of Context-Enabled Applications. In *Proceedings of the SIGCHI Conference on Human Factors in Computing Systems: the CHI is the Limit*, 1999.

[SDW08] Choonsun Shin, Anind K. Dey, and Woontack Woo. Mixed-Initiative Conflict Resolution for Context-Aware Applications. In *Proceedings of the 10th International Conference on Ubiquitous Computing*, 2008.

[SEC] Ltd. Samsung Electronics Co. Galaxy S III Specification. http://www.samsung.com/global/galaxys3/specifications.html. accessed 20.10.2012.

[SF94] Daniel Sabin and Eugene C. Freuder. Contradicting Conventional Wisdom in Constraint Satisfaction. In *Proceedings of the 2nd International Workshop on Principles and Practice of Constraint Programming (PPCP)*, 1994.

[SG94] Rok Sosic and Jun Gu. Efficient Local Search With Conflict Minimization: A Case Study of the n-Queens Problem. *IEEE Transactions on Knowledge and Data Engineering*, 6(5):661–668, 1994.

[SG02] Joao Pedro Sousa and David Garlan. Aura: An Architectural Framework for User Mobility in Ubiquitous Computing Environments. In *Proceedings of the IFIP 17th World Computer Congress - TC2 Stream / 3rd IEEE/IFIP Conference on Software Architecture: System Design, Development and Maintenance*, 2002.

[SHW05] Choonsung Shin, Daeho Han, and Woontack Woo. Conflict Management for Media Services by Exploiting Service Profiles and User Preference. In *Proceeding of the 1st International Workshop on Personalized Context Modeling and Management for UbiComp Applications*, 2005.

[SLS05] Evi Syukur, Seng Wai Loke, and Peter Stanski. Methods for Policy Conflict Detection and Resolution in Pervasive Computing Environments. In *Proceedings of the 14th International World Wide Web Conference, Policy Management for the Web*, 2005.

[SRL10] Thais R.M. Braga Silva, Linnyer B. Ruiz, and Antonio A.F. Loureiro. Towards a Conflict Resolution Approach for Collective Ubiquitous Context-Aware Systems. In *Proceedings of the 12th International Conference on Information Integration and Web-based Applications & Services*, 2010.

[SS77] Richard M. Stallman and Gerald J. Sussman. Forward Reasoning and Dependency-Directed Backtracking in a System for Computer-aided Circuit Analysis. *Artificial Intelligence*, 9(2):135–196, 1977.

[SvdZH08] Andreas Schroeder, Marjolein van der Zwaag, and Moritz Hammer. A Middleware Architecture for Human-Centred Pervasive Adaptive Applications. In *Proceedings of the 2nd IEEE International Conference on Self-Adaptive and Self-Organizing Systems Workshops*, 2008.

[SW05] Choonsung Shin and Woontack Woo. Conflict Resolution Method utilizing Context History for Context-Aware Applications. In *Proceedings of the 1st International Workshop on Exploiting Context Histories in Smart Environments*, 2005.

[SW09] Choonsung Shin and Woontack Woo. Service Conflict Management Framework for Multi-User Inhabited Smart Home. *Journal of Universal Computer Science*, 15(12):2330–2352, 2009.

[SYW07] Choonsun Shin, Hyoseok Yoon, and Woontack Woo. User-Centric Conflict Management for Media Services Using Personal Companions. *ETRI*, 29(3):311–321, 2007.

[TJK+08] G.S. Thyagaraju, S.M. Joshi, Umakant P. Kulkarni, S.K. NarasimhaMurthy, and Anil R. Yardi. Conflict Resolution in Multiuser Context-Aware Environments. In *Proceedings of the International Conference on Computational Intelligence for Modelling Control & Automation*, 2008.

[TSB06] Verena Tuttlies, Gregor Schiele, and Christian Becker. End-user Configuration for Pervasive Computing Environments. In *Proceedings of the International Conference on Complex, Intelligent and Software Intensive Systems*, 2006.

[VMG+01] Kirsi Virrantaus, Jouni Markkula, Artem Garmash, Vagan Terziyan, Jari Veijalainen, Artem Katanosov, and Henry Tirri. Developing GIS-Supported Location-Based Services. In *Proceedings of the 2nd International Conference on Web Information Systems Engineering*, 2001.

[VVV08] Antti-Matti Vainio, Miika Valtonen, and Jukka Vanhala. Proactive Fuzzy Control and Adaptation Methods for Smart Homes. *IEEE Intelligent Systems*, 23(2):42–49, mar 2008.

[Wal75] David Waltz. Understanding Line Drawings of Scenes with Shadows. In *The Psychology of Computer Vision*, 1975.

[Wal00] Toby Walsh. SAT vs. CSP. In *Principles and Practice of Constraint Programming – CP 2000*, volume 1894 of *Lecture Notes in Computer Science*, pages 441–456. Springer Verlag, 2000.

[Wei91] Mark Weiser. The Computer for the 21st Century. *Scientific American*, 265(3):66–75, 1991.

[Wf] Standard Wi-fi. http://standards.ieee.org/about/get/802/802.11.html. IEEE 802.11 - 2012, accessed 30.09.2012.

[WKM07] Michael Wilson, Mario Kolberg, and Evan H. Magill. Considering Side Effects in Service Interactions in Home Automation - an Online Approach.

In *Proceedings of the International Conference on Feature Interactions in Software and Communication Systems*, 2007.

[WSA+95] Roy Want, Bill N. Schilit, Norman I. Adams, Rich Gold, Karin Petersen, David Goldberg, John R. Ellis, and Mark Weiser. An Overview of the PARCTAB Ubiquitous Computing Experiment. *Personal Communications*, 2:28–43, 1995.

[WZGP04] Xiao Hang Wang, Da Qing Zhang, Tao Gu, and Hung Keng Pung. Ontology based context modeling and reasoning using owl. In *Proceedings of the 2nd IEEE Annual Conference on Pervasive Computing and Communications Workshops*, 2004.

ENTSCHEIDUNGSUNTERSTÜTZUNG FÜR ÖKONOMISCHE PROBLEME

Herausgegeben von Christian Becker, Wolfgang Gaul, Armin Heinzl,
Alexander Mädche und Martin Schader

Band 1 Ingo Böckenholt: Mehrdimensionale Skalierung qualitativer Daten. Ein Instrument zur Unterstützung von Marketingentscheidungen. 1989.

Band 2 Jürgen Joseph: Arbeitswissenschaftliche Aspekte der betrieblichen Einführung neuer Technologien am Beispiel von Computer Aided Design (CAD). Felduntersuchung zur Ermittlung arbeitswissenschaftlicher Empfehlungen für die Einführung neuer Technologien. 1990.

Band 3 Eva Schönfelder: Entwicklung eines Verfahrens zur Bewertung von Schichtsystemen nach arbeitswissenschaftlichen Kriterien. 1992.

Band 4 Michael Bargl: Akzeptanz und Effizienz computergestützter Dispositionssysteme in der Transportwirtschaft. Empirische Studien zur Implementierungsforschung von Entscheidungsunterstützungssystemen am Beispiel computergestützter Tourenplanungssysteme. 1994.

Band 5 Reinhold Decker: Analyse und Simulation des Kaufverhaltens auf Konsumgütermärkten. Konzeption eines modell- und wissensorientierten Systems zur Auswertung von Paneldaten. 1994.

Band 6 Wolfgang Gaul / Martin Schader (Hrsg.): Wissensbasierte Marketing-Datenanalyse. Das WIMDAS-Projekt. 1994.

Band 7 Daniel Baier: Konzipierung und Realisierung einer Unterstützung des kombinierten Einsatzes von Methoden bei der Positionierungsanalyse. 1994.

Band 8 Ulrich Lutz: Preispolitik im internationalen Marketing und westeuropäische Integration. 1994.

Band 9 Kirsten Petersen: Design eines Courseware-Entwicklungssystems für den computerunterstützten universitären Unterricht. CULLIS-Teilprojekt I. 1996.

Band 10 Stefan Neumann: Einsatz von Interactive Video im computerunterstützten universitären Unterricht. CULLIS Teilprojekt II. 1996.

Band 11 Eberhard Aust: Simultane Conjointanalyse, Benefitsegmentierung, Produktlinien- und Preisgestaltung. 1996.

Band 12 Peter Heydebreck: Technologische Verflechtung. Ein Instrument zum Erreichen von Produkt- und Prozeßinnovationserfolg. 1996.

Band 13 Michael Pesch: Effiziente Verkaufsplanung im Investitionsgütermarketing. 1997.

Band 14 Frank Wartenberg: Entscheidungsunterstützung im persönlichen Verkauf. 1997.

Band 15 Thomas Lechler: Erfolgsfaktoren des Projektmanagements. 1997.

Band 16 Alexandre Saad: Anbahnung und Erfolg von europäischen kooperativen F&E-Projekten. Eine empirische Analyse anhand von ESPRIT-Projekten. 1998.

Band 17 Michael Löffler: Integrierte Preisoptimierung. 1999.

Band 18 Frank Säuberlich: KDD und Data Mining als Hilfsmittel zur Entscheidungsunterstützung. 2000.

INFORMATIONSTECHNOLOGIE UND ÖKONOMIE

(Neuer Reihentitel ab Band 19)

Band 19 Rainer Kiel: Dialog-gesteuerte Regelsysteme. Definition, Eigenschaften und Anwendungen. 2001.

Band 20 Axel Korthaus: Komponentenbasierte Entwicklung computergestützter betrieblicher Informationssysteme. 2001.

Band 21 Markus Aleksy: Entwicklung einer komponentenbasierten Architektur zur Implementierung paralleler Anwendungen mittels CORBA. Mit Beispielen aus den Wirtschaftswissenschaften. 2003.

Band 22 Michael Zapf: Flexible Kundeninteraktionsprozesse im Communication Center. 2003.

Band 23 Yvonne Staack: Kundenbindung im eBusiness. Eine kausalanalytische Untersuchung der Determinanten, Dimensionen und Verhaltenskonsequenzen der Kundenbindung im Online-Shopping und Online-Brokerage. 2004.

Band 24 Lars Schmidt-Thieme: Assoziationsregel-Algorithmen für Daten mit komplexer Strutkur. Mit Anwendungen im Web Mining. 2003.

Band 25 Stefan Hocke: Flexibilitätsmanagement in der Logistik. Systemtheoretische Fundierung und Simulation logistischer Gestaltungsparameter. 2004.

Band 26 Viktor Jung: Markteintrittsgestaltung neugegründeter Unternehmen. Situationsspezifische und erfolgsbezogene Analyse. 2004.

Band 27 Lars Brehm: Postimplementierungsphase von ERP-Systemen in Unternehmen. Organisatorische Gestaltung und kritische Erfolgsfaktoren. 2004.

Band 28 Ralf Gitzel: Model-Driven Software Development Using a Metamodel-Based Extension Mechanism for UML. 2006.

Band 29 Bernd Stauß: Optimale Gestaltung von Auswahlmenüs und deren Verwendung im Variantenmanagement. 2006.

Band 30 Nils Schumacher: EDI via XML. Potentiale und Strategien für global orientierte kleine und mittlere Unternehmen. 2007.

Band 31 Christian Cuske: Quantifizierung operationeller Technologierisiken bei Kreditinstituten. Eine Ontologie-zentrierte Vorgehensweise im Spannungsfeld bankinterner und aufsichtsrechtlicher Sichtweise. 2007.

Band 32 Matthias Merz: Konzeptioneller Entwurf und prototypische Implementierung einer Sicherheitsarchitektur für die Java Data Objects-Spezifikation. 2008.

Band 33 Tobias Hildenbrand: Improving Traceability in Distributed Collaborative Software Development. A Design Science Approach. 2008.

Band 34 Karen H. L. Tso-Sutter: Towards Metadata-Aware Algorithms for Recommender Systems. 2010.

Band 35 Thomas Schoberth: Eine Längsschnittstudie der Kommunikationsaktivität in virtuellen Gemeinschaften. 2010.

Band 36 Nima Mazloumi: Entwurf eines Referenzmodells und Frameworks zur Erstellung hybrider Lehr- und Lernszenarien. Mit Fallbeispielen aus der Betriebswirtschaftslehre und der Wirtschaftsinformatik. 2010.

Band 37 Anja Zöller: Effizienzanalyse grundlegender Gestaltungsgrößen der OP-Organisation. 2010.

Band 38 Jessica Katharina Winkler: International Entry Mode Choices of Software Firms. An Analysis of Product-Specific Determinants. 2009.

Band 39 Martin J. Lafleur: *Loyalty Profiling*. Erfolgsdimensionen und Modellansätze eines effizienten und effektiven Customer Relationship Management. 2010.

Band 40 Ingo Ott: Effizientes Prozessmanagement im öffentlichen Dienst. 2010.

Band 41 Stefan Seedorf: Ontologie-gestützte Entwicklung komponentenbasierter Anwendungssysteme. Ein wissensbasiertes Informationssystem zur Unterstützung der Entwicklung und Wartung von Geschäftskomponenten (KompIS). 2010.

Band 42 Dominic Gastes: Erhebungsprozesse und Konsistenzanforderungen im Analytic Hierarchy Process (AHP). 2011.

Band 43 *erscheint in Kürze*

Band 44 Olaf Thiele: Informationsvisualisierungen auf mobilen Endgeräten zur Unterstützung des betrieblichen Datenmanagements. 2011.

Band 45 Krisztian Antal Buza: Fusion Methods for Time-Series Classification. 2011.

Band 46 Thomas Kude: The Coordination of Inter-Organizational Networks in the Enterprise Software Industry. The Perspective of Complementors. 2012.

Band 47 Alexandra Rebecca Klages: Clusteranalyse für Netzwerke. 2012.

Band 48 Christian Thum: Enabling Lightweight Real-time Collaboration. 2012.

Band 49 Miroslav Lazic: The Impact of Information Technology Governance on Business Performance. 2013.

Band 50 Verena Elisabeth Majuntke: Application Coordination in Pervasive Systems. 2013.

www.peterlang.de